DESTINATION INDIANA

TRAVELS THROUGH HOOSIER HISTORY

DESTINATION INDIANA

TRAVELS THROUGH HOOSIER HISTORY

TEXT BY

RAY E. BOOMHOWER

PHOTOGRAPHY BY

DARRYL JONES

INDIANA HISTORICAL SOCIETY   INDIANAPOLIS 2000

The paper in this publication meets the minimum requirements of
American National Standard for Information Sciences—Permanence of Paper
for Printed Library Materials, ANSI Z39.48-1984. ∞

Library of Congress Cataloging-in-Publication Data

Boomhower, Ray E., 1959-
    Destination Indiana: travels through Hoosier history / text by Ray E. Boomhower;
photography by Darryl Jones.
        p. cm.
    ISBN 0-87195-147-9 (cloth)
    1. Historic sites—Indiana. 2. Historic sites—Indiana—Pictorial works. 3. Indiana—
History, Local. 4. Indiana—History, Local—Pictorial works. I. Jones, Darryl L., 1948-
II. Title.
F527.B66 2000
977.2—dc21   00-032018
                                                                                        CIP

For J. Kent Calder and Megan McKee, two editors who always

showed an "accommodating spirit" to this writer

CONTENTS

Ray E. Boomhower

The summer 1990 issue of the Indiana Historical Society's popular history magazine *Traces of Indiana and Midwestern History* featured within its forty-eight pages a distinctive blend of articles on the culture and heritage of the nineteenth state, including pieces on such prominent figures from the Hoosier State's past as author Gene Stratton-Porter, politician Wendell Willkie, artist T. C. Steele, and businessman Eli Lilly. The issue also marked the inaugural appearance of what was to become a fixture in the magazine: a department titled "Destination Indiana." The column, which in this instance examined the then new Indiana Basketball Hall of Fame in New Castle, went on through the years to examine a wealth of historic sites open to the public in Indiana and earned a distinction as one of the magazine's most popular features.

That first column on the Hall of Fame marked a milestone for me, as it was the first of what came to be many appearances in the magazine. The idea for the column, and its characteristic name, came about as the result of a partnership between myself and the magazine's staff, in particular J. Kent Calder, managing editor, and Megan McKee, editor. The column's success owes much to both of these fine editors, not the least of which was their help with naming the department for the year-old publication. Before deciding on "Destination Indiana," we considered and rejected such titles as: "Off the Beaten Path," "Indiana Highways," "Indiana Almanac," "You Can't Get There from Here," "Wandering Indiana," "This Is Indiana," "Hoosier Byways," and "Exit: Indiana." Both editors also ably assisted me in the sometimes painful process of learning how to write for a history magazine. That first column on the Basketball Hall of Fame owed much to my experience as a former reporter for the *Rensselaer Republican* and *Anderson Herald* and consisted mainly of an interview with its then executive director, J. Ronald Newlin. In subsequent issues, the editors and I worked to produce the blending of biographical and architectural detail that has made the department a success.

For the past ten years it has been my pleasure to research and write "Destination Indiana" for *Traces*, and in addition visit the fascinating historic sites that dot the Hoosier landscape. In determining what sites to highlight in the magazine, the editors and I used as a guide one main criterion: the site must be open to the public on a regular basis. We also attempted, as best we could, to highlight every region of the state.

On my travels researching and visiting sites throughout Indiana, I have relished meeting and working with the knowledgeable and helpful curators and volunteers who keep the story of the state's past alive for today's Hoosiers. With their assistance, I have been able to inform the magazine's readers about the life and times of the people who not only inhabited these architectural wonders but also breathed life into them—George Ade, Indiana's "warmhearted satirist," at Hazelden in Brook; Ernie Pyle, the GI's friend, at the Ernie Pyle State Historic Site in Dana; William Henry Harrison, Indiana Territory governor and hero of the Battle of Tippecanoe, at Grouseland in Vincennes; Elisabeth Ball, poet and

conservationist, at Oakhurst Gardens in Muncie; and many others. By knowing more about the people who lived and died in these buildings, and writing about their lives for *Traces*, I have learned that these structures are more than just beautiful examples of architecture. I hope readers of this book realize it too and that they are inspired to discover more about their state's past.

The twenty-five sites featured in this book may have different design features, but they do have one thing in common: the dedicated staff who ensure that these places are available for all to enjoy. In particular I wish to thank the following for their help in the past with the column in *Traces* and this book: Catherine Bohls, Huddleston Farmhouse; Peggy Brooks, Colonel William Jones State Historic Site; Joellen Bye, Culbertson Mansion State Historic Site; David Cart, Kate Branigan, and Jane Campbell, Lanier Mansion State Historic Site; Sandy Crain, James Whitcomb Riley Home (Indianapolis); Phyllis Geeslin, President Benjamin Harrison Home; Owen Glendening, Minnetrista Cultural Center; Kathleen Gray, Ruthmere Mansion; Lorethea Hamke, Grouseland; Evelyn Hobson, Ernie Pyle State Historic Site; Jeffrey Huntington, Hillforest Mansion; Saundra Jackson, Levi Coffin State Historic Site; Kate Jones, Corydon Capitol State Historic Site; Charles King, Eugene V. Debs Foundation; Katherine McDonell and Oren Cooley, Indiana Medical History Museum; Andrea Smith, T. C. Steele State Historic Site; Becky Smith, Limberlost State Historic Site; Joann Spragg, General Lew Wallace Study and Ben-Hur Museum; Margie Sweeney, Gene Stratton-Porter State Historic Site; Kelly Thompson, Howard County Historical Society; and Connie Weinzapfel, Historic New Harmony.

Also providing invaluable assistance and advice on the column and this book have been the following Indiana Historical Society staff: Thomas A. Mason, Publications Division director; Paula Corpuz, senior editor; Shirley McCord, editor; Kathy Breen, assistant editor; and George Hanlin, assistant editor. Editing, as writer John Jerome once observed, "always hurts" because it is painful for authors to have their creations (already perfect in their eyes) improved upon. All of the IHS staff worked to ensure that the process for this book was a painless one.

As she has with countless Society books, Pat Prather of Dean Johnson Design contributed her stellar design skills in helping craft the book you hold in your hands. Book design is an art, and nobody practices the art better than Pat.

Of course, the project could not have been accomplished without the fine work of photographer Darryl Jones. The images he captured at the twenty-five sites help bring these structures to life and help us imagine the lives that were lived in each one.

The inspiration for my writing these past ten years has been my wife, the aforementioned Megan McKee. Without her to serve as my ablest supporter and severest critic, none of this would have been possible. To her, I owe everything.

In North Carolina in the early 1800s a Quaker child came face-to-face with the institution of slavery. One day while he was out with his father chopping wood by the side of a road, a group of slaves, handcuffed and chained together, passed by on their way to be sold in Georgia, Alabama, and Louisiana. Questioned by the young boy's father about why they were chained, one of the men sadly replied, "They have taken us away from our wives and children, and they chain us lest we should make our escape and go back to them." After the dejected company left the scene, the youth wondered to himself how he would feel if his father were taken away from him.

The incident by the side of the road marked the first awakening of Levi Coffin's sympathy with the oppressed, which, he observed in his memoirs, together with a strong hatred of oppression and injustice in any form, "were the motives that influenced my whole after-life." Coffin, who moved to the Indiana town of Newport (now Fountain City) in 1826 and became an important merchant there, acted on his beliefs. From his simple eight-room house in Wayne County, and with the help of his wife, Catharine, he managed over the next twenty years to offer a safe haven to thousands of African Americans fleeing slavery's evils on the Underground Railroad along major escape routes leading from Cincinnati, Madison, and Jeffersonville. "Seldom a week passed," said Coffin, "without our receiving passengers by this mysterious road. We found it necessary to be always prepared to receive such company and properly care for them." Coffin's efforts won for him the designation "President of the Underground Railroad" and for the Coffins' home the title "Grand Central Station" on the slaves' path to freedom in the north and Canada. Legend has it that one of the refugees who found shelter in the Coffins' home was later immortalized as the character Eliza, the heroine of Harriet Beecher Stowe's classic novel, *Uncle Tom's Cabin*.

A state historic site under the Indiana State Museum System, the Levi Coffin house was placed on the National Register of Historic Places in 1966 by the U.S. Department of the Interior. The state purchased the Coffin house in 1967 and leased it to the Wayne County Historical Society. The society, after generous donations from the community and the Lilly Endowment, renovated the structure and opened it to the public as a museum in 1970. Today, volunteers from the Levi Coffin House Association offer tours of the Federal-style brick home built in 1839 (the Coffins'

fourth home in Newport). The home's fireplaces, floors, doors, and most of the woodwork are original. The furnishings all predate 1847 and as nearly as possible are typical of a Quaker family and of the time period.

Levi Coffin was born on 28 October 1798 on a farm in New Garden, North Carolina, the only son of seven children born to Levi and Prudence (Williams) Coffin. Because his father could not spare him from work on the farm, young Levi received the bulk of his education at home, under instruction from his father and sisters. His home schooling proved to be good enough for Coffin to find work as a teacher for several years. He shared with his relatives an abhorrence for slavery. "Both my parents and grandparents were opposed to slavery," Coffin noted in his reminiscences, published in 1876, "and none of either of the families ever owned slaves; and all were friends of the oppressed, so I claim that I inherited my anti-slavery principles."

While he was still a teenager, Coffin had his first opportunity to offer assistance to a slave. Attending a cornhusking, the fifteen-year-old Coffin noticed a group of slaves brought to the husking by a slave dealer named Stephen Holland. While the other whites in the party dined, the Quaker boy remained behind to talk with the slaves and to "see if I could render them any service." He learned that one of the slaves, named Stephen, was freeborn and a former indentured servant to Edward Lloyd, a

Philadelphia Quaker, but later had been kidnapped and sold into slavery. Thinking fast, Coffin arranged with a "trusty negro, whom I knew well," to take Stephen the next night to his father's house. After learning the particulars of the now slave's case, the elder Coffin wrote Lloyd of his former servant's plight, and eventually Stephen was liberated from slavery in Georgia.

In 1821, with his cousin Vestal Coffin, Levi Coffin ran a Sunday school for blacks at New Garden, where the slaves were taught to read using the Bible. Alarmed slave owners, however, soon forced the school to close. Coffin, who married Catharine White, a woman he had known since childhood, on 28 October 1824, decided two years later to join family members who had moved to the young state of Indiana. Establishing a store in Newport, Coffin prospered, expanding his operations to include cutting pork and manufacturing linseed oil. His business success led to him being elected director of the State Bank's Richmond branch.

Even with his busy life as a merchant, Coffin was "never too busy to engage in Underground Railroad affairs." In fact, his business success aided him immeasurably in helping slaves to freedom. "The Underground Railroad business increased as time advanced," he said, "and it was attended with heavy expenses, which I could not have borne had not my affairs been prosperous." Also, his thriving business and importance in the community helped deflect opposition to his Underground Railroad activities from proslavery supporters and slave hunters in the area. Questioned by others in the community about why he aided slaves when he knew he could be arrested for his activities, Coffin told them that he "read in the Bible when I was a boy that it was right to take in the stranger and administer to

those in distress, and that I thought it was always safe to do right. The Bible, in bidding us to feed the hungry and clothe the naked, said nothing about color, and I should try to follow out the teachings of that good book."

The fearlessness the Coffins displayed in offering assistance to the fleeing slaves had an effect on their neighbors. Levi Coffin noted that those who had once "stood aloof from the work" eventually contributed clothing for the fugitives and aided the Coffins in forwarding the slaves on their way to freedom but were "timid about sheltering them under their roof; so that part

of the work devolved on us." Fugitives came to the Coffins' home at all hours of the night and announced their presence by a gentle rap at the door. "I would invite them, in a low tone," said Coffin, "to come in, and they would follow me into the darkened house without a word, for we knew not who might be watching and listening." Once safely inside, the slaves would be fed and made comfortable for the evening. The number of fugitives varied considerably through the years, Coffin noted, but annually averaged more than one hundred.

In 1847 Coffin left Newport to open a wholesale ware-

house in Cincinnati that handled cotton goods, sugar, and spices produced by free labor. The enterprise had been funded a year earlier by a Quaker Convention at Salem, Indiana. Coffin and his wife continued to help slaves via the Underground Railroad while living in Cincinnati. Both during and after the Civil War, Coffin served as a leading figure in the Western Freedman's Aid Society, which helped educate and provide in other ways for former slaves. Working for the freedman's cause in England and Europe, Coffin in one year raised more than $100,000 for the society. In 1867 he served as a delegate to the International Anti-Slavery Conference in Paris. He died on 16 September 1877 in Cincinnati and is buried in that city's Spring Grove Cemetery.

Located at 113 U.S. 27 North in Fountain City, the Levi Coffin State Historic Site is open from 1:00 P.M. to 4:00 P.M. Tuesday through Saturday (1 June through 31 August) and from 1:00 P.M. to 4:00 P.M. on Saturday (1 September through 31 October). For more information, write the site at P.O. Box 775, Fountain City, IN 47341; or call (765) 847-2432.

The War of 1812 was going badly for America in the winter of 1813 when the Indiana Territory's general assembly met in the territorial capital of Vincennes. Although the war created financial difficulties for the legislature, a greater problem was brewing—which city would have the honor of becoming the new territorial capital? Forces opposed to former territorial governor William Henry Harrison, who had left the state to help fight the British, wanted to remove the capital from Harrison's Knox County stronghold. A number of cities—Charlestown, Clarksville, Jeffersonville, Lawrenceburg, and Madison (which offered to donate $10,000 if the legislators located the capital there)—were considered before the lawmakers decided on Corydon.

Corydon's selection, according to the *Western Gazetteer*, caused "great dissatisfaction in other parts of the state." To forestall any interference with the orderly transfer of the capital, the general assembly gave the territorial governor the power to call out the militia to provide for the "safe conveyance of any books, papers, or other thing by this act made necessary to be conveyed to the said town

of Corydon." The move was made officially on 1 May 1813, and the tiny hamlet served as the center of government for Indiana until 1 January 1825, when the capital was moved to Indianapolis.

The unpretentious square, Federal-style limestone building that served as the state's first capitol (described by historian Jacob Piatt Dunn, Jr., as "a rather imposing building for the time in Indiana") began life as the Harrison County courthouse. The building's stewards today, however, are not judges but another governmental authority, the Indiana State Museum System. The ISMS maintains the structure as a state historic site, along with the nearby Gov. William Hendricks Headquarters.

In the early nineteenth century the town of Corydon was "an easy-going, old-fashioned Virginia village, with an ambition to be decent and to cultivate the social spirit," according to Charles Moores, an

Indiana Historical Commission member writing in 1917. The town occupied land purchased by William Henry Harrison in 1804; he named the town after his favorite song, "The Pastoral Elegy," which laments the death of a young shepherd, Corydon. One of the leading figures in the town's early history was Dennis Pennington, former speaker in the lower house of the territorial legislature who had come to the area in the early 1800s. Known as a devoted champion of Harrison County, Uncle Dennis, as he

was called, played a key role in securing for Corydon its distinction as state capital.

A carpenter and contractor by trade, Pennington represented Harrison County at the 1813 session of the Indiana Territory's general assembly. Maneuvering behind the scenes, Pennington suggested Corydon as the perfect site for the next capital, noting that a new courthouse being constructed there could be used as the territory's capitol. This new structure, however, was not

completed very quickly. Although Corydon became the capital in May 1813, the courthouse was not ready for occupancy until 1816. Pennington supervised construction for the $3,000 structure, which was expensive compared to the $500 log courthouse other counties were constructing.

During the flurry of building activity in Corydon, the Indiana Territory had reached the necessary sixty thousand population to be considered for statehood. Forty-three delegates were elected for a constitutional convention, which met in Corydon from 10 through 29 June 1816. Some sessions were held in the new courthouse, but because of the oppressive summer heat, others were organized beneath the shade of a massive elm tree (now known as the Constitutional Elm) located just a short distance away. Delegates approved the new constitution on 29 June 1816, and six months later President James Madison signed legislation designating Indiana the nineteenth state of the Union.

The initial Indiana General Assembly met in the Corydon capitol on 4 November 1816. Space was tight in the two-story building, as the representatives, senators, and lieutenant governor had to share space with the three supreme court judges, some of

Gov. Jonathan Jennings's officers, the county court, and the county clerk. A bigger concern to legislators during subsequent years was the cost for boarding in and around Corydon during the sessions. The *Indiana Gazette* in December 1820 noted that the "old famous resolution to remove the legislature to Charleston or some other place where it is imagined members can get boarding lower than Corydon is going the formal rounds of legislation, when it is understood that no more is intended by it than to beat down the prices of boarding." Prices for boarding, fixed by the county commissioners, were 37½ cents for breakfast or dinner, 12½ cents for lodging, and 37½ cents a quart for whiskey.

Corydon's reign as the heart of Indiana government drew to a close in 1820 when the legislature appointed a commission to find a new site for the state capital. In the fall of 1824 Samuel Merrill, state treasurer, led a group of wagons carrying the state's records and finances on the 125-mile trip from Corydon to Indianapolis. With the loss of its status as state capitol, the Corydon building reverted to a full-time Harrison County courthouse.

During the renewed interest in state history spawned by the Indiana centennial celebration in 1916, plans were made to preserve the old state capitol. In 1917 the general assembly passed an act to purchase the structure "as a memorial to the pioneers who established the Commonwealth of Indiana." In the late 1920s the old capitol was restored to its original appearance.

The Corydon Capitol State Historic Site is open from 9:00 A.M. to 5:00 P.M. Tuesday through Saturday and from 1:00 P.M. to 5:00 P.M. on Sunday. The site is closed mid-December to mid-March. For more information, write the site at 202 E. Walnut St., Corydon, IN 47112; or call (812) 738-4890.

Early in the nineteenth century thousands of people pulled up stakes and set off for new opportunities in the young state of Indiana. Many of these newcomers to the Hoosier State settled in communities established along pioneer transportation routes, especially river towns such as Madison and New Albany. One of the many who settled in New Albany was William Stewart Culbertson, who had been an apprentice in a dry goods store in his home state of Pennsylvania. In just a few years, Culbertson, who started his own dry goods business in 1841, had made his fortune. Although his former business is gone, his three-story, twenty-five-room, Second Empire–style residence, Culbertson Mansion, remains as a reminder of the Gilded Age lifestyle of the Victorian era.

The Culbertson Mansion, now a state historic site in the Indiana State Museum System, also represents what a community can accomplish when it sets out to preserve its past. In 1964, with plans afoot to construct a service station on the mansion site, citizens banded together to form Historic New Albany, Inc., bought the property for $25,000, and worked to restore the mansion to its original

Victorian grandeur. The organization, which donated the property to the state in 1976, succeeded; with its hand-painted ceilings, carved rosewood staircase, marble fireplaces, and crystal chandeliers, the Culbertson Mansion reflects the affluence of a man once considered to be the wealthiest in Indiana.

Born in New Market, Pennsylvania, in 1814, Culbertson was the second of six children and the eldest son of a family headed by William Culbertson. At the age of fifteen, Culbertson left New Market for Harrisburg, Pennsylvania, where he served as an apprentice in a dry goods business owned by Abener Oves. With his apprenticeship finished in 1835, Culbertson, with a glowing recommendation from his employer, left Pennsylvania for the new lands in the West. He eventually settled in New Albany, a thriving Ohio River community, and obtained a job as a clerk in a store owned by Alexander Burnett.

Fueled by ambition and with a savvy for business, Culbertson moved on to become copartner and business manager for the firm Downey and Keyes. In 1841, a year after his marriage to Eliza Vance of Corydon, Culbertson, in partnership with his younger brother John, opened his own dry goods business as Culbertson & Brother. Over the years his business thrived, helped in part by the Civil War. A perhaps apocryphal story states that the Culbertson firm had purchased fifty carloads of Southern cotton processed at the Cannelton cotton mills and sold it to Crane, Springdale & Company. The New York firm, however, could not ship the cotton to its intended market in England and subsequently returned it to Culbertson. By the time the cotton made its way back to New Albany, the price for the scarce commodity had skyrocketed, and Culbertson sold the product for a substantial profit.

Although Culbertson had become rich through his business ventures, which also included real estate, banking, railroads, and other businesses, he suffered a personal tragedy when his wife died in January 1865 of typhoid pneumonia at age forty-three, leaving her husband to care for the couple's six children. Two years after his wife's death, Culbertson married Cornelia Warner Eggleston, a widow from Evansville. (Cornelia died in 1880, and Culbertson was married for a third time in 1884 to Rebecca Keith Spears Young, a Kentucky widow.) Along with his marriage, Culbertson undertook another new venture with the construction of a home on a lot he had purchased four years earlier for $5,000. Built between 1867 and 1869, the home, which cost $120,000 to build, became one of the largest in southern Indiana. James and William Banes of New Albany, contractors for the project, used approximately twenty-five thousand semicircular bricks to make the rounded bay windows for the Second Empire home. In

1870 Culbertson purchased the lot next door on which his son Samuel's house was built from 1885 to 1886. With the purchase, Culbertson owned an entire city block.

None of the original furnishings for the home survives today, nor are there any photographs of the mansion's interior. A 29 June 1878 article in the *New Albany Ledger-Standard*, however, did include a bit of detail about the Culbertson home. "The drawing room," the newspaper noted, "is certainly a marvel of beauty, the upholstery is in pale blue satin of the richest texture, and the curtains of the finest lace. Upon the walls are some of the most beautiful and exquisite paintings of the most gifted artists." Five years later, the newspaper, on the occasion of the marriage of one of Culbertson's daughters, described the home as being "rich in carved furniture," having "great bay windows" and "magnificent crystal chandeliers in the drawing room."

Along with his fine home and varied business interests, Culbertson became well respected in the community for his philanthropic works. In 1873 he established a home for indigent widows in New Albany, an approximately fifteen-room structure costing $25,000. Following his wife Cornelia's death from cholera

in 1880, and in memory of her concern for the city's orphans, Culbertson spent $22,000 to construct the Cornelia Memorial Orphan's Home. Although the Orphan's Home was torn down in 1963, the Widow's Home (later known as the Old Ladies' Home) stands in New Albany today as a private residence.

Culbertson, who in his lifetime amassed a personal fortune valued at $3.5 million, died of congestive heart failure on 25 June 1892 at age seventy-eight. Culbertson's widow, Rebecca, lived in the mansion for several years but eventually put the property, including a carriage house, and its furnishings up for auction. John McDonald, a former Culbertson business partner, bought the home in hopes of turning it into a hospital. Those plans failed, however, and McDonald and his family lived in the mansion until his death in 1945. The following year McDonald's daughter sold the home to American Legion Post #28, which used the property for parties, meetings, receptions, and other community events. Citing the financial drain imposed by maintaining such a structure, the post sold the building to Historic New Albany, which worked for a number of years to restore the mansion before donating it to the state.

In 1980–81, and again in 1989, the state made extensive renovations to the structure, including making the mansion's exterior more closely resemble its original nineteenth-century appearance. Today, visitors to the Culbertson Mansion can tour its grand parlors, dining room, and bedrooms, and also the kitchen and laundry room.

The Culbertson Mansion State Historic Site is open from 9:00 A.M. to 5:00 P.M. Tuesday through Saturday and from 1:00 P.M. to 5:00 P.M. on Sunday. The site is closed to the public from mid-December to mid-March. For more information, write the site at 914 E. Main St., New Albany, IN 47150; or call (812) 944-9600.

EUGENE V. DEBS HOME

Terre Haute

Convict Number 9653 was a model prisoner at the federal penitentiary in Atlanta, Georgia, in 1920. Hardened criminals and prison officials alike were touched by his friendliness and concern for all. The son of immigrant parents, he dropped out of high school at age fourteen to work as a painter in the Terre Haute railroad yards for fifty cents a day. In spite of this humble background, and his incarceration in a prison cell, Convict 9653 received nearly one million votes as the Socialist party's presidential candidate in 1920.

The prisoner was Hoosier union organizer, writer, lecturer, and five-time presidential hopeful Eugene V. Debs. Although during his life his beliefs were frequently out of step with those of his Terre Haute neighbors and the country, many of Debs's "radical" reforms—an eight-hour workday, pensions, workman's compensation, sick leave, and social security—are commonplace in today's workplace. His philosophy was contained in the short statement: "While there is a lower class, I am in it; While there is a criminal element, I am of it; While there is a soul in prison, I am not free!"

Debs's vision is kept alive by the Eugene V. Debs Foundation, which is headquartered in the former home of Debs and his wife, Katherine Metzel, in Terre Haute. Built in 1890 at the cost of $4,500, the two-and-a-half-story Victorian frame dwelling, named a National Historic Landmark in 1966, contains a treasure trove of Debs memorabilia.

Debs was born on 5 November 1855, the eldest son of parents who came to Indiana in 1851 from Alsace. Leaving school to help his financially strapped family, Debs found a job scraping paint off railroad cars. Shortly after, he moved up to become a locomotive fireman. Concerned about their son's safety, Debs's family members urged him to quit, and in 1874 Debs moved on to a clerking job at the Hulman & Cox wholesale grocery firm.

Even with his new job, Debs retained his interest in the railroad workers' plight. On 27 February 1875 he became a charter member and the secretary of the Vigo Lodge, Brotherhood of Locomotive Firemen. By 1880 Debs had become grand secretary of the national Brotherhood of Locomotive Firemen and editor of the *Locomotive Fireman's Magazine*. Also during this time Debs became active in Democratic politics, serving two terms as Terre Haute city clerk and one frustrating term in the Indiana legislature as state representative. During his service in the general assembly,

Debs supported or drafted bills for woman's suffrage, the abolishment of racial distinctions, and compensation for railroad workers; all met with defeat. He refused to run for reelection.

In June 1893 Debs helped found the first industrial union in the United States, the American Railway Union, which was open to all railroad employees. During its first full year in operation, the union won a major and peaceful victory in its strike against the Great Northern Railway. The union next became involved in a sympathy strike in support of employees of the George Pullman company, maker of Pullman railroad cars. Approximately one hundred thousand workers went on strike, halting all railroad traffic in and out of Chicago except trains carrying U.S. mail.

The bitter Pullman strike, often known as the "Debs Rebellion," ended when President Grover Cleveland sent in federal troops. For his refusal of a court order to end the strike, Debs and seven other American Railway Union officials, dubbed the "Woodstock Eight," were convicted (despite being represented by Clarence Darrow) for contempt of court. During his six-month stay in the Woodstock, Illinois, jail, Debs converted to the socialist cause.

In 1900 in Indianapolis the Social Democratic party held its first national convention and nominated Debs as its presidential candidate—a role he would also fill in the 1904, 1908, 1912, and 1920 presidential elections. In his first

run for the White House, Debs captured 86,935 votes. That total rose to 402,489 votes four years later.

For the 1908 election Debs took his campaign on the road, traveling coast to coast in his "Red Special" train, which consisted of a locomotive with a coach, sleeper, and baggage car packed with campaign literature. Debs spoke to some five hundred thousand people on his journey, many of whom paid to be able to hear his speeches—a far cry from today's campaigns. In spite of his whirlwind efforts, however, Debs was able to capture only 17,891 more votes than his 1904 total.

The 1912 election was the high-water mark for the Socialist party as 900,369 people, approximately 6 percent of the total vote, marked their ballots for Debs. Four years later, seeing war fever building in the country, Debs declined to run for president and instead tried unsuccessfully for a post in Congress. His congressional campaign saw Debs speaking forcefully against the war then raging in Europe, a stance he maintained as America entered the war on the Allied side in 1917.

On 16 June 1918 Debs spoke out against the war in a speech in Canton, Ohio. Federal authorities were quick to react, arresting

the labor leader later that month in Cleveland and charging him with violating the Espionage Act. During his trial the prosecution argued that Debs, in his Canton speech, had tried to discourage enlistment in the armed forces and promoted insubordination in the ranks. Speaking in his own defense, Debs admitted making the speech, but he denied the prosecution's allegations and challenged the validity of the Espionage Act, claiming it violated the constitutional right to free speech. In two hours of testimony before the jury, Debs had this to say about his Canton speech and beliefs: "In what I had to say there my purpose was to have the people understand something about the social system in which we live and to prepare them to change this system by perfectly peaceable and orderly means into what I, as a Socialist, conceive to be a real democracy. . . . I am doing what little I can, and have been for many years, to bring about a change that shall do away with the rule of the great body of the people by a relatively small class and establish in this country an industrial and social democracy."

On 14 September 1918 Judge D. C. Westenhauer issued his sentence, sending Debs to prison for ten years. An appeal by Debs to the U.S. Supreme Court failed, and in April 1919 he entered the Moundsville, West Virginia, state prison (which housed some federal detainees) to begin serving his jail term. Two months later he was transferred to the Atlanta federal prison from which he ran his fifth and final presidential campaign. In the 1920 election Debs captured his highest vote total ever (913,664), but the Socialist party's total vote percentage dropped to 3 percent.

On Christmas Day in 1921, the man who defeated Debs for president, Warren G. Harding, commuted his sentence to time served, and Debs returned home to Terre Haute. Although Debs continued to speak and write for the socialist cause during the next few years, he was in poor health due to his prison experience and the effects of his grueling work schedule throughout his adult life. He died in Lindlahr sanitarium just outside of Chicago on 20 October 1926. In his history of Indiana, Hoosier historian

John Bartlow Martin noted that Debs "was in the main stream of Indiana protest, the ceaseless quest for the better life begun by Robert Owen, the uprising against authority begun in William Henry Harrison's time. . . . They left an impress and a heritage,—Debs most of all. He was the greatest of the Indiana protestants, the most effective."

During his many years on the campaign trail, on lecture tours, and in jail cells, there was one constant in Debs's life: his home in Terre Haute. The eight-room, seven-fireplace house hosted a variety of famous figures of the period, including James Whitcomb Riley. In fact, Riley was such a frequent visitor that the guest bedroom was named in his honor.

In 1962 plans were made to demolish the home and convert the land into a parking lot. The Eugene V. Debs Foundation, however, hurriedly organized, acquired the home for $9,500, and began extensive restoration work. Today, the eight rooms on the first and second floors contain period furniture, family photographs and memorabilia, campaign posters and buttons, correspondence from such figures as Riley, Upton Sinclair, and Carl Sandburg, and even the keys to the cell and cell block from Debs's Woodstock imprisonment and the table he used as a desk at Moundsville prison. The third floor, formerly an unfinished attic, contains both an auditorium and murals featuring scenes from Debs's life painted by Terre Haute artist John Laska.

The Eugene V. Debs Home, located at 451 N. Eighth St. in Terre Haute, is open to the public from 1:00 P.M. to 4:30 P.M. Wednesday through Sunday. For more information, write the Eugene V. Debs Foundation at P.O. Box 843, Terre Haute, IN 47808; or call (812) 232-2163.

The summer of 1810 was a tense one in Vincennes, capital of the decade-old Indiana Territory. Although territorial governor William Henry Harrison had successfully negotiated treaties that opened approximately three million acres to settlement, Northwest Territory tribes—encouraged by the British—were rallying to the call of the Shawnee warrior Tecumseh and his brother, the Prophet, to end the white man's intrusion onto their land.

To help calm the situation, Governor Harrison arranged a meeting with Tecumseh, who arrived in Vincennes on 12 August, accompanied by anywhere from one hundred to four hundred (accounts differ on the number) of his braves. After eight days of discussion, the two sides were unable to come to terms and eventually settled their differences on the battlefield. The scene of this remarkable meeting between two leading figures in Indiana and American history—the stately grounds of Harrison's home, known as Grouseland—matched the grandeur of its participants.

Years after that fateful meeting, Hoosiers can tour the Federal-style mansion, preserved through the efforts of the Francis Vigo Chapter of the Daughters of the American Revolution, and experience the gracious living enjoyed by the hero of the Battle of Tippecanoe and ninth president of the United States.

On 13 May 1800, at the age of twenty-seven, William Henry Harrison was selected by Federalist president John Quincy Adams to serve as governor of the Indiana Territory. For a salary of $2,000 per year, Harrison governed land that would be carved into the present-day states of Illinois, Indiana, Michigan, Minnesota, and Wisconsin. Harrison held his post as governor for four three-year terms.

At the time of Harrison's first administration, Vincennes, the seat of the new government for the Indiana Territory, numbered approximately seven hundred citizens, both French and American. Reaching Vincennes on 10 January 1801 to assume his office, Harrison was a guest at the home of Col. Francis Vigo, a leading citizen of the village. However, Harrison did start planning for a home of his own. In a letter to a friend, James Findlay of Cincinnati, Harrison noted that he had "purchased a farm of about 300 acres joining the town which is all cleared. I am now engaged in fencing it and shall begin to build next spring if I can find the means."

Assured of a second term as territorial governor by President Thomas Jefferson, Harrison turned his attention to the construction of his new home. Built between 1803 and 1804, Grouseland (believed to be the first brick building in Vincennes and the Indiana Territory) matched the stately homes on the James River that Harrison knew from his childhood in Virginia. As James A. Green notes in his book *William Henry Harrison: His Life and Times*, Harrison had "built a house that would have done credit to the spacious times of Old Virginia. It was of brick, two stories, with a high roof and dormer windows. In contrast with the one story log cabins of the period it was palatial. Most of the frontiersmen had never seen such a magnificent mansion and to the Indians it surely appeared as a veritable miracle of construction."

Reputed to have cost $20,000 to build, Grouseland was constructed of bricks manufactured not far from the town. Harrison is said to have paid for the bricks with a large parcel of land. The house and the dependency to the rear were joined by a covered passage. Grouseland's six large bedrooms had to accommodate the Harrisons and their eight children.

Along with the sounds of children, the home also reverberated with the sounds of political discussions, as Governor Harrison often invited legislators to stay at the mansion. Although Harrison was unsuccessful in arranging a treaty with Tecumseh, five of the eight land-ceding treaties the governor negotiated with other tribes between 1803 and 1809 were signed by him at Grouseland.

The Harrison family moved from Grouseland during the summer of 1812, and the home was occupied by Judge Benjamin Parke. In 1819 Harrison's eldest son, John Cleves Symmes Harrison, was appointed receiver of the land office in Vincennes, and two years later the house was deeded to him. John Harrison, his wife Clarissa, and their six children lived in Grouseland for about ten years before passing it on to heirs, who retained ownership until the 1850s.

After passing out of the Harrison family's hands, the mansion was used for a variety of purposes, including a warehouse for storing wheat (by John Myers, a grain dealer), a private residence,

and a hotel. In 1909 the Vincennes Water Company purchased the home. The firm planned to raze the structure and use the site for a settling tank.

Hearing of Grouseland's plight, the Francis Vigo Chapter of the Daughters of the American Revolution campaigned to save the home. By 1916 the chapter had raised $2,000 from the community and was given a limited deed to the property. In 1935 the city purchased the water company and a year later gave the DAR a quitclaim deed to Grouseland.

Since rescuing the mansion from the wrecking ball and open-

ing it to the public as a historical museum in 1911, the DAR has painstakingly restored the home and furnished it with Harrison possessions and period pieces. Costumed volunteer tour guides lead visitors through the mansion and discuss such features as the self-supporting stairway in the entrance hall; the parlor or council chamber where Harrison signed the Treaty of Grouseland; the shutter with a bullet hole in it, supposedly fired by a Native American hoping to kill Harrison; and the legend of an under-ground passage from the basement to the Wabash River.

Grouseland is located in Vincennes at the Harrison Historical Park on the northwest corner of Park and Scott Streets. The mansion is open daily from 9:00 A.M. to 5:00 P.M. In January and February the hours are from 11:00 A.M. to 4:00 P.M. For more information, write Grouseland at 3 W. Scott St., Vincennes, IN 47591; or call (812) 882-2096.

On a fall day in 1888 the sound of marching feet echoed through the streets of Indianapolis. Armed with red, white, and blue parasols and led by drummers from eleven states, a crowd of approximately forty thousand commercial travelers marched up North Delaware Street to call upon a local lawyer, who happened to be the Republican nominee for president. As the attorney and his wife appeared at the front door of their sixteen-room Italianate Victorian mansion, the travelers responded with "cheers upon cheers," one eyewitness, Mary Lord Dimmick, remembered later. The cheers lasted until the attorney spoke, she said, and "then . . . you could have heard a pin drop."

The crowds that flocked to Indianapolis in 1888 came to visit a man who, from an early age, seemed destined for political life. Benjamin Harrison was the son of John Scott Harrison, a two-term congressman from Ohio; grandson of William Henry Harrison, the first governor of the Indiana Territory and ninth president of the United States; and the great-grandson of Benjamin Harrison V, governor of Virginia and a signer of the Declaration of Independence. Benjamin

Harrison captured the presidency that year, defeating incumbent Grover Cleveland. The excitement engendered by those heady days of Indiana political power are showcased in the President Benjamin Harrison Home, a National Historic Landmark, where the memory of the Hoosier favorite son is perpetuated by the President Benjamin Harrison Home Foundation.

The twenty-third president was born on his grandfather's farm at North Bend, Ohio, on 20 August 1833. After receiving his early education at Farmers' College in Cincinnati, Harrison graduated from Miami University in Oxford, Ohio, in 1852. He then studied law for two years with a Cincinnati firm and married Caroline Lavinia Scott, an Oxford Female Institute graduate and an accomplished artist and musician. In 1854 the twenty-one-year-old Harrison and his wife moved to the growing city of Indianapolis, and Harrison established his own law practice. Given Hoosiers' love of politics, and the famous Harrison name, the young lawyer became drawn—somewhat reluctantly—into the political scene. In 1856 while busy working at his law office, Harrison was interrupted by some Republican friends who dragged him from his office to speak before a political gathering. Introduced to the crowd as the grandson of Old Tippecanoe, Harrison firmly replied: "I want it understood that I am the grandson of nobody. I believe that every man should stand on his own merits."

The Harrison family's strong political background, however, did aid young Harrison as he undertook a political career, becoming Indianapolis city attorney in 1857 and being elected to the post of Indiana Supreme Court reporter three years later. The Civil War halted Harrison's political career. Asked by Indiana governor Oliver P. Morton to recruit men for the 70th Regiment, Indiana Volunteers, Harrison served as a colonel with that outfit and offered sterling service to the Union cause in the battles of Peachtree Creek and Resaca, Georgia. During the war Harrison received the nickname Little Ben from his troops (he stood five feet, six inches tall), a sobriquet "which in their understanding connoted courage and daring," noted Harrison biographer Harry J. Sievers.

Mustered out of the army with a brevet brigadier general's commission, Harrison returned to Indianapolis to fill out his term as supreme court reporter before returning to his private law practice. Paradoxically for Harrison, his biographer Sievers noted, the financial panic that gripped the country in the early 1870s actually aided his firm as "defaults, mortgage foreclosures, and bankruptcy cases flooded the office." Financially secure, Harrison turned his attention to building a new home for his family, which included at that time two teenaged children, Russell and Mary. In 1867 Harrison had purchased at auction a double lot on North Delaware Street,

and it was here that the family's new red-brick home was built during the fall and winter of 1874 and 1875 at a cost of approximately $20,000. Along with a library for Harrison's substantial book collection, the home possessed a ballroom and became a popular location for society events, including Thursday afternoon teas hosted by Caroline Scott Harrison, who later became the first president-general of the Daughters of the American Revolution.

In 1876 Harrison returned to the political arena, running as the GOP candidate for Indiana governor. He lost to Democrat James "Blue Jeans" Williams; his electoral failure, however, did not hurt his strong standing with Hoosier Republicans. In 1881 the Indiana legislature, controlled by the GOP, elected Harrison to serve a six-year term in the U.S. Senate. Harrison arrived on the scene at a time when Indiana played a prominent role in national affairs. To attract Hoosier voters, political parties often selected favorite sons from Indiana to bolster the parties' chances in November. In 1888 the GOP nominated Harrison as its presidential candidate. Like most presidential contenders of that time, Harrison refused to barnstorm around the country for votes, preferring instead to remain at home. "I have a great risk

of meeting a fool at home," he told journalist Whitelaw Reid, "but the candidate who travels cannot escape him." During the election, Harrison, from his front stoop, gave more than eighty speeches to the approximately three hundred thousand citizens who visited the home. Although Harrison received about one hundred thousand fewer popular votes than Cleveland, the Hoosier politician carried the electoral college and captured the presidency.

Despite an inauspicious beginning to his term (even many Republican supporters considered him a cold fish), Harrison signed into law during his administration such significant legislation as the Sherman Antitrust Act and the McKinley Tariff, presided over the admission of six western states into the Union in 1889 and 1890, and established thirteen million acres of land for forest reserves and national parks. Also during his four years in office, Congress, for the first time except during

wartime, appropriated a billion dollars. Criticized by Democrats for such lavish spending, House Speaker Thomas Reed responded, "this is a billion-dollar country." While in office Harrison suffered a great personal loss when his beloved wife died on 25 October 1892. Renominated by the Republicans, Harrison was nevertheless defeated for reelection by his old foe Cleveland in 1892. After his defeat Harrison returned to Indianapolis, reopened his lucrative law practice, and married his late wife's niece, Mary Lord Dimmick. He died in 1901 and is buried in Indianapolis's Crown Hill Cemetery.

Although used for a time as a dormitory for women by the Jordan Conservatory of Music, today the President Benjamin

Harrison Home is open to the public as a museum and houses some 3,700 artifacts and 2,440 books. Many of the home's artifacts belonged to the Harrison family, including White House china designed by Caroline Harrison. The home's third floor, originally a ballroom, now is used as a changing exhibition gallery. Textiles, dresses, and other artifacts are displayed throughout the house.

The President Benjamin Harrison Home is open from 10:00 A.M. to 3:30 P.M. Monday through Saturday and from 12:30 P.M. to 3:30 P.M. on Sunday. Guided tours begin every thirty minutes and last approximately one hour. For more information, write the site at 1230 N. Delaware St., Indianapolis, IN 46202; or call (317) 631-1898.

The 1908 presidential contest pitted two would-be reformers against each other. In June in Chicago the Republicans nominated William Howard Taft, groomed for the post by former president Theodore Roosevelt. The Democrats responded by selecting William Jennings Bryan, who would be making his third, and last, attempt for the nation's highest office. And while Bryan was shocked by his staggering million-vote loss to Taft at the polls, perhaps the campaign's biggest surprise came at the beginning when Taft decided to open his race for the White House in the small Indiana town of Brook.

Brook may have been a tiny dot on Indiana's map, but it did have something other Hoosier towns did not: the spacious country estate of Indiana journalist, playwright, and "warmhearted satirist," George Ade. Hazelden Farm was the scene of a number of large parties and celebrations in the thirty-nine years Ade resided there; enough, in fact, that Ade's biographer recalled it being described as the "amusement center of the United States." Ade himself noted in an autobiographical piece: "I love to put on big parties or celebrations and see a throng of people having a good time."

The spirit of laughter and fun of those Ade soirees of yesteryear is reflected in the work of the George Ade Memorial Association, which is responsible for Hazelden. Located just fifteen miles from Ade's birthplace in Kentland, the farm is listed on the National Register of Historic Places and offers a window into the world of the man known as the Aesop of Indiana.

Born on 9 February 1866, Ade was the second youngest of seven children raised by John and Adaline (Bush) Ade. "From the time I could read," Ade remembered later in life, "I had my nose in a book, and I lacked enthusiasm for manual labor." His aversion to physical work, especially his dislike for farming, troubled his father, who wondered how his son would make a living. In 1883 Ade started classes at Purdue University. His attention, however, soon focused on the Grand Opera House in Lafayette, where he became a regular patron— sometimes to the detriment of his studies. Ade noted that he was a "star student as a Freshman but wobbly later on and a total loss in Mathematics." Still, while at the university he did meet and begin a lifelong friendship with Hoosier cartoonist John T. McCutcheon.

After graduating from Purdue in 1887 with a bachelor of science degree, Ade started work as a reporter for the *Lafayette Call* at the princely sum of six dollars per week. Along with his low salary, Ade had to cope with a frugal editor, who, for example, liked to use old envelopes as copy paper. Ade later moved on to a job writing testimonials for a patent medicine company's tobacco-habit cure. In recalling Ade's work for the firm, McCutcheon noted that the cure was not a fake remedy, "for it was guaranteed to cure the most persistent tobacco habit if the tobacco user followed the directions. The first direction was to discontinue the use of tobacco and then take the tablets."

By 1890 Ade had joined McCutcheon on the staff of the *Chicago Morning News*. Ade's first regular assignment was a daily weather story. His big break came when the steamer *Tioga* exploded on the Chicago River and, because no other reporters were available, he rushed to the scene and produced the best account of the tragedy. His success led to his covering such important events as the heavyweight championship fight between John L. Sullivan and James J. "Gentleman Jim" Corbett in New Orleans and the 1893 Chicago World's Fair. In November 1893 Ade was put in charge of the column "Stories of the Streets and of the Town," which also featured McCutcheon's illustrations. In his writing Ade captured life on Chicago's bustling streets through the antics of such characters as Artie, a young office boy; Doc' Horne, a "gentlemanly liar"; and Pink Marsh, a shoeshine boy in a barbershop. Ade's column was also the birthplace of the work that made him famous: fables.

Fables in Slang, published in 1899, became an immediate hit with the public, selling

sixty-nine thousand copies that year alone. These "modern fables" were syndicated nationally, produced as movies by the Essanay Film Company, and turned into comic strips by cartoonist Art Helfant. Kansas newspaper editor William Allen White was moved to write that he "would rather have written *Fables in Slang* than be President." Despite such lavish attention, Ade remained levelheaded, wryly noting: "By a queer twist of circumstances I have become known to the general public as a 'humorist' and a writer of 'slang'. I never wanted to be a comic or tried to be one. The playful vernacular and idiomatic talk of the street and the fanciful figures of speech which came out for years under the heading 'Fables in Slang' had no relation whatever to the cryptic language of the underworld or the patois of the criminal element. Always I wrote for the 'family trade' and I used no word or phrase which might give offense to mother and the girls or a professor of English."

Ade next turned his humorist's pen to the theater, writing his first Broadway play, *The Sultan of Sulu*, a comic opera about America's activities in the Philippines, in 1902. Other hit plays soon followed, including *Peggy from Paris*, a musical comedy; *The County Chairman*, a drama about small-town politics; and his best-known play, *The College Widow*, a comedy about college life and football set on the Wabash College campus in Crawfordsville, Indiana.

While Ade was busy writing and traveling, frequently abroad, back home in Indiana his brother William was acquiring on Ade's behalf numerous acres of farmland in Newton County. In 1902 William Ade bought 417 acres near the town of Brook. Impressed by the wooded land, George Ade called on his friend Billy Mann, a Chicago architect, to design a small dwelling for him that would cost $2,500. A suggestion here and a suggestion there later, Ade ended up with an impressive English Manor/Tudor–style home that cost approximately $25,000. Ade, who moved into his Hazelden Farm estate in the summer of 1904, described his home as "about the size of a girl's school, with added wings for the managers, otherwise known as employees." Included with the home and elaborate gardens were a swimming pool, greenhouse, barn, caretaker's cottage, fuel supply house, and forty-foot-tall water tank.

Once settled into his new home, Ade wasted little time in making his neighbors feel welcome, hosting numerous parties. Along with Taft's visit, Hazelden was the site of celebrations for the Indiana Society of Chicago, Purdue University alumni, and local children. Ade also hosted a rally for Theodore Roosevelt's Bull Moose party in 1912; a homecoming for soldiers and sailors on 4 July 1919; and a party and speech for vice presidential candidate Charles G. Dawes in 1924. It was McCutcheon who best captured the spirited, and crowded, times at his friend's home when he noted: "If all the Sigma Chis, Purdue students, Indiana friends, movie stars, stage stars, political mass meetings, golf professionals and automobile clubs from Chicago, Indiana, New York and Hollywood, who have eaten the famous fried chicken at Hazelden farm, being regaled the while by the stories of one of the greatest American raconteurs, were stood in a row, the line would reach from hell to breakfast."

Ade died on 23 May 1944 in Brook after an illness of many months. Following his death Hazelden was turned over to Purdue University. Unable to afford its upkeep, the university turned the site over to the state, which also could not afford to maintain the home and in turn gave it to Newton County. In 1962 Hazelden was acquired by the George Ade Memorial Association, formed that same year in Kentland. The association raised the necessary funds to renovate the home and restore a number of rooms to their original condition. Memorabilia from Ade's life is displayed in the home.

Hazelden, located east of Brook on Highway 16, is open for visitation by appointment. For more information, write the George Ade Memorial Association at P.O. Box 388, Kentland, IN 47951; or call (219) 275-4011.

On a late spring afternoon in 1853 the steamer *Forest Queen* out of Cincinnati glided to a stop at a dock in the Hoosier river town of Aurora. Among its passengers that day was Isaiah Rogers, an architect known as the "father of the modern hotel." Rogers, however, was not in town to design a new hotel but rather to meet with Thomas Gaff, a prominent Aurora financier and industrialist, and examine a plot of land on which Gaff wished to build a new home. In the two days Rogers was in town, he not only reviewed the proposed homesite with Gaff but also was "well entertained," taking a walk with his new client and discussing with him a number of subjects. "Had a very pleasant day," Rogers noted in his daybook.

Rogers designed on ten acres of land overlooking the Ohio River a magnificent mansion that Gaff and his family would call home from 1855 to 1891. Although based on the Italian Renaissance architectural style, the two-story home's design reflected Gaff's involvement in the shipping industry with its full-width frontal porch reminiscent of a steamboat's deck. The enduring legacy of Rogers's design for what came to be known as Hillforest Mansion was evidenced in 1992 when the U.S. Department of the Interior informed the Hillforest Historical Foundation, Inc., which owns and operates the home, that it had been designated as a National Historic Landmark.

Thomas Gaff, the original owner of this magnificent edifice, was born near Edinburgh, Scotland, on 8 July 1808. Gaff came to the United States with his parents, James and Margaret Gaff, at the age of three, settling in Springfield, New Jersey. As a young man Gaff learned papermaking from his father and the distilling business from a Brooklyn uncle, Charles Wilson. In partnership with his brothers James and John, Thomas Gaff

opened a distillery in Philadelphia that was soon a success. The panic of 1837, however, had the brothers looking for new opportunities elsewhere. Reportedly offered tax incentives and land, the brothers decided to move their business to Aurora; James arrived in 1841, Thomas in 1843, and John in 1845.

In 1843 Thomas and James established the T. and J. W. Gaff & Company distillery on the banks of Hogan Creek, one block north of downtown Aurora. The distillery produced bourbon, rye, and Thistle Dew scotch whiskey. The Gaffs also owned the Crescent Brewing Company, which featured Aurora Lager Beer. The beer's quality was so high that it was exported to Germany. Along with their brewing interests, the brothers were involved in a number of other businesses, including farming, Nevada silver mines, a Cincinnati jewelry store, foundry and machine works, turnpike and canal construction, and two Louisiana plantations. Their mill in Columbus, Indiana, produced "Cerealine," which was touted as the first ready-made cereal in the world.

With their heavy reliance on the Ohio River for shipping, the Gaff brothers also owned a fleet of steamboats that they used to transport their distillery and brewery products. During the Civil War the Gaffs furnished these steamboats and other supplies for the Union cause. One of their steamboats, the *Forest Queen*, became headquarters for Maj. Gen. William Tecumseh Sherman during the Siege of Vicksburg. The steamboat, under the command of Capt. C. D. Conway of Aurora, successfully ran the Vicksburg blockade but

was burned to the water by Confederates in Saint Louis, Missouri.

In addition to their many business ventures, the Gaff brothers were heavily involved in civic affairs, backing the town's first utility company, the Aurora Gas and Coke Company, and founding in 1856 the First National Bank of Aurora, which Thomas served as president. Thomas also helped to organize Aurora's school system, served on the city council with his brother James (John was mayor), incorporated Riverview Cemetery, and, with his brothers, bought Aurora a fire engine and town clock.

An 1880 history of Indiana's eminent and self-made men captured Thomas Gaff's wide range of interests, both business and civic, by noting: "As a financier, he is regarded as one of the best in the country. His executive ability is remarkable. No transaction within the range of his complicated affairs escapes his observation. He is generous, and ready to relieve the deserving poor. Few men have been more liberal in the contributions to religious and charitable objects."

Thomas was not the first Gaff brother to build a home in Aurora. His brother James had that distinction, constructing on the southwest corner of Fourth and Main Streets a home known as Linden Terrace, named for the Linden trees he imported from Germany for landscaping. Thomas, however, would more than match his brother's efforts with Hillforest, which was built into a hillside in the manner in which Renaissance villas in Italy were built into the mountains. The building's steamboat-influenced style is reflected in its circular porches and colonnades, curved doors and windows, and a circular rooftop belvedere with round-arched windows that resemble a steamboat's pilothouse. Also, the interior features a flying staircase in the entrance hall that is typical of the better steamboats of the time period.

Thomas Gaff enjoyed the comforts of his stately mansion until his death on 25 April 1884. The home remained in the Gaff family until 1926, when it was purchased by Will Stark, a local furniture manufacturer. The home eventually became the clubhouse for the local chapter of the Veterans of Foreign

Wars, which used it for that purpose from the late 1940s to the mid-1950s. In late 1955, when the VFW decided the home did not meet its needs, local citizens, fearing the home would meet the same fate as Linden Terrace (which had fallen into disrepair and had been torn down), banded together to purchase the mansion. They formed the Hillforest Historical Foundation as a nonprofit organization dedicated to the home's restoration and preservation. Hillforest has been open to the public as a historic property museum since 1956.

Located at the top of Main Street at Fifth Street in Aurora off U.S. 50, Hillforest is open to the public from 1:00 P.M. to 5:00 P.M. Tuesday through Sunday, 1 April through 30 December. The mansion is also open on Monday from Memorial Day to Labor Day. For more information, write the Hillforest Historical Foundation at P.O. Box 127, Aurora, IN 47001; or call (812) 926-0087.

Farmer and lapsed Quaker John Huddleston was worried. A party of immigrants that had stopped at his Wayne County, Indiana, farmhouse the night before had departed at daybreak and left behind bread they had baked in the oven at the Huddleston farm, which had become a regular stopping point for travelers on the National Road. "Hastily saddling a horse," according to Lee Burns in his history of the National Road in Indiana, "he [Huddleston] followed them with the bread only to discover that their hurried departure had been caused by the fact that they had taken his best set of harness."

Recalling the adventures and everyday life of a family that lived along a roadway called the Appian Way of America (U.S. 40 to today's travelers) is the Huddleston Farmhouse Inn Museum's mission. The three-story, Federal-style brick home, which is listed on the National Register of Historic Places, is now the Historic Landmarks Foundation of Indiana's responsibility. Purchased by the organization in 1966, the farmhouse and its outbuildings have been restored; visitors can experience why weary travelers were eager to stop and rest there.

Born in 1807 near Greensboro, North Carolina, John Huddleston grew up in a farming family. He was eight years old when his Quaker family migrated from North Carolina to Union County, Indiana, as part of the "great Quaker Migration," one of many such waves of migration by Quakers to eastern Indiana during the early nineteenth century. In March 1830 Huddleston married fellow Quaker Susannah Moyer in her parents' home a few miles east of Liberty, Indiana. Soon after his marriage, Huddleston was disowned by the Quaker Yearly Meeting for "disunity" with the religion's discipline. The couple lived in Union County until 1835, when Huddleston, an early Hoosier entrepreneur, decided to take advantage of a new highway just completed to Indianapolis—the National Road.

The idea for a roadway linking eastern manufacturers with western markets was first broached by George Washington as early as 1755. It took until 1802, however, for the idea to take shape. Congress, in the act it passed creating Ohio, provided that 5 percent of the funds received by the federal government from public land sales in the state would be used to build public roads from the Atlantic Ocean to Ohio. Similar provisions were placed into the acts incorporating the states of Indiana, Illinois, and Missouri. In 1803 Congress made the first appropriation for a highway across the Allegheny Mountains to Ohio—the National Road. Beginning in Cumberland, Maryland, and running through six states, the road cost approximately $7 million.

The National Road, also called the National Pike, the Old Pike, and the Cumberland Road, was an immediate hit with immigrants, freight wagoners, express carriers, and mail coach drivers. "The road became a busy thoroughfare," noted Burns. "Wagon house yards were located along the line, where the tired horses rested over night beside their great loads, and taverns, famous in their day, were built at convenient points for the stages, that were constantly arriving and departing." Not everyone, however, was pleased with the road's quality. A familiar chant about the National Road in Indiana went:

The roads are impassable—
Hardly jackassable;
I think those that travel 'em
Should turn out and gravel 'em.

The National Road in Indiana traveled due west from the Ohio state line to Indianapolis, passing through such Hoosier cities as Richmond and Centerville, and on to Terre Haute. Huddleston became one of many in Indiana who tried to wring a financial advantage out of the road. Along with his parents and many of his brothers' and sisters' families, he moved his young family to the town of Dublin. In 1838 Huddleston bought seventy acres along the National Road, just west of Cambridge City. His new farm included four acres with frontage along the highway.

The Huddlestons lived in a log house on their farm while a new brick house, barn, and outbuildings were being erected. The 125,000 bricks used for the buildings were fired on-site, and the lumber and stone used in construction were

taken from the land and nearby quarries. The Huddleston farm was built to be more than a place for raising crops—it was set up to serve travelers. The barn had extra stalls for tired draft animals, the house contained two basement kitchens for rental by families, and the smokehouse, outdoor oven, and outhouse were all scaled to serve travelers as well as the family.

Although convenient for travelers, the Huddleston farm's accommodations were far from plush. Families bought food to prepare in the public kitchens or paid to eat at the Huddlestons' table. In bad weather travelers slept in the barn, on the house's porches, or in its lower level. Usually they slept in their wagons parked in the barnyard. The Huddleston family's living quarters were on the house's upper two floors.

The former Quaker did well in his new home. By the time the federal agricultural census was taken in 1850 he had one of the most productive farms in the township, producing twenty tons of hay, two hundred pounds of cheese, and one hundred pounds of butter. Along with his farming and lodging business, Huddleston helped support his large family by carting goods to and from Cincinnati and working on the National Road. Family histories

state that Huddleston refused to carry tobacco or liquor on his trips to and from the city. They also report that his work on the road consisted of grading the long hill on Dublin's east side.

John Huddleston died in 1877 from complications resulting from an injury sustained when a family horse kicked him in the head. His wife, Susannah, died in 1892. The children divided the estate equally. After being sold out of the Huddleston family in 1934, the farm served many purposes; at various times it was a rental property, an antique store, and a restaurant. In the 1960s Eli Lilly, Indianapolis pharmaceutical businessman and philanthropist, became interested in helping save the Huddleston farm. With his guidance and a generous gift, Historic Landmarks Foundation, a nonprofit organization that encourages and participates in a number of statewide preservation projects, was able to buy the farm in 1966.

Today's visitors to the Huddleston Farmhouse Inn Museum can enjoy permanent and rotating exhibitions on the history of the house, the National Road, and architecture in eastern Indiana. The museum also sponsors reenactments and workshops for both adults and children.

The Huddleston Farmhouse Inn Museum is located on U.S. 40 on Cambridge City's western edge and is open from 10:00 A.M. to 4:00 P.M. Tuesday through Saturday, February through December. In addition, the farm is open from 1:00 P.M. to 4:00 P.M. Sunday, May through August. For more information, write the museum at P.O. Box 284, Cambridge City, IN 47327; or call (317) 478-3172.

The reporter from the *Indianapolis Sentinel* was impressed. Just the night before he had witnessed "imposing" dedication ceremonies for a new building at the Central Indiana Hospital for the Insane on Indianapolis's near west side. A two-story brick building, which was intended for use by physicians and medical students to study diseases of the mind and nervous system, had opened to great fanfare. Calling it one of the most complete laboratories in the country and the world, the reporter went on to write in the *Sentinel*'s 19 December 1896 edition that "physicians who have studied in the pathological laboratories of the old world say that they have seen nothing to surpass it."

The structure that amazed the newspaper reporter of yesteryear continues to draw rave notices today as the home of the Indiana Medical History Museum, which is housed in the Old Pathology Building. The museum, a nonprofit organization established in 1969 to preserve the historic structure, has received national recognition. Dr. Martin J. Lipp, in his book *Medical Landmarks USA: A Travel Guide*, calls the institution, which is listed on the National Register of

Historic Places, "a marvelous museum . . . quite simply without peer in the entire country. This is a pristine, turn-of-the-century research building."

The Old Pathology Building has played an important role in medical history from its first days until the present. When it opened, the building housed the largest research facility in the state—even larger than the laboratories at Indianapolis City Hospital or the medical colleges. Today, it stands as the oldest surviving pathology building in the country.

The Old Pathology Building's origins date back to the 1870s, when mental-hospital physicians were increasingly under fire by critics for a lack of sufficient training in psychiatry and neurology. In response, mental hospitals began to hire pathologists for their staffs and to create facilities for research and training. On 31 October 1894 Dr. George F. Edenharter, the new Central Indiana Hospital superintendent, unveiled plans for a structure designed "for the use of physicians and medical students of the State, wherein the diseases of the mind and nervous system could be clinically studied and, if possible, determine their causes and formulate methods for their prevention and cure."

Building such a structure, however, would not be an easy task. "It is hard to convince the average legislature," said Dr. H. M. Lash, a member of Indianapolis's medical society, "that the insane are entitled to much and legislators are apt to look with the most favor on the annual report that shows the least expenditure."

It took nearly two years, but Edenharter was able to get the job done—with design help from Indianapolis architect Adolph Scherrer. Scherrer, whose work included such sites as the state capitol and the Indianapolis Athletic Club, designed a two-story brick structure with nineteen "working rooms." With total costs reaching $18,000, the Pathology Building included a large amphitheater-style lecture hall, library, autopsy rooms, a photography room, and three laboratories.

The building contained, for that time, state-of-the-art research facilities and laboratory equipment for the scientific

study of mental illness. "Indiana has taken a great step in the scientific investigation of the causes and cures of insanity," Dr. Ludwig Hektoen, a Chicago pathologist, said of the building. Also impressive was the structure's interior, as cabinets, woodwork, and laboratory tables were all made of white oak. Brass fixtures and copper and tile trim adorned laboratory tables.

Although the building received lavish praise, original research there did not start until the 1920s. The Pathology Building, however, did provide medical schools with a facility for teaching neurology and psychiatry. In 1900 two private medical schools, the Medical College of Indiana (affiliated with Purdue University) and the Central College of Physicians and Surgeons, conducted formal classes in the building's amphitheater. By 1908 the faculties of the two medical schools were merged with the Indiana University School of Medicine, which continued holding psychiatry and neurology classes in the building until 1956.

An important part of the scientific work conducted in the structure was the systematic performance of autopsies. The autopsies helped physicians correlate unusual behavioral patterns with internal abnormalities. Such procedures were performed in

the building's mortuary. While the hospital's pathologist did the autopsy, one of the physicians assisted him and another recorded the postmortem details.

Bodies for use in the mortuary were stored in a small building cooled with ice—known as the "dead house"—located next to the Pathology Building. Because of the lack of cadavers for use in medical schools at the time, body snatching, especially from graveyards at state mental hospitals, was common. To guard against such an occurrence, special cages, or "wire corpse protectors," were locked over bodies stored in both the mortuary and the dead house to prevent their removal.

Perhaps the most noteworthy work at the building occurred during the 1920s and 1930s when research was conducted on central-nervous-system syphilis, one of the major causes of institutionalization in the late nineteenth and early twentieth centuries. Pathologist Walter Bruetsch, who joined the hospital's staff in 1925, researched the disease and its effect on the nervous system—work that gained him international renown.

Central State Hospital (as it was renamed), now closed, used the building as a laboratory and classroom until the mid-1960s. In 1969 the Indiana Medical History Museum was established to maintain the historic structure and the collection of more than fifteen thousand medical and health-care artifacts. The museum's collections include diagnostic instruments, surgical equipment, pharmaceutical bottles, dental equipment, patent medicines, and "quack cure" devices. The museum also has more than three thousand medical volumes and a growing collection of portraiture and medical artwork.

The Indiana Medical History Museum is located in the Old Pathology Building on the grounds of the former Central State Hospital. The museum is open from 10:00 A.M. to 4:00 P.M. Wednesday through Saturday. For more information, write the museum at 3045 W. Vermont St., Indianapolis, IN 46222; or call (317) 635-7329.

Shortly after the end of the 1875 Indiana legislative session, a state senator, Andrew J. Boone, died at his home in Lebanon. The death of this one legislator was of more than usual concern to his constituents and fellow lawmakers because some argued that Boone's fatal illness was due to the structure where the state's laws were being made: the Indiana State Capitol. The first statehouse constructed in Indianapolis, completed in 1835 at a cost of approximately $60,000, had deteriorated over the years to the point that one representative, Richard R. Stephenson of Hamilton County, likened the building to the Black Hole of Calcutta. The New State House Committee, appointed by the Indiana General Assembly in 1873, had warned lawmakers that the building was "totally inadequate to the public service." Something had to be done before more legislators were felled by the structure's leaky roof, poor ventilation, and crumbling walls.

On 14 March 1877 the general assembly finally acted to rectify the situation, approving an act authorizing the construction of a new statehouse at a cost not to exceed $2 million. Despite losing the original architect for the project, Edwin

May, who died only a few years after work had started, construction on the new state capitol, an example of the Renaissance Revival style, was completed on 2 October 1888 at a total expense of $1,980,969, well within the state's original budget. The statehouse, with architecture reminiscent of the U.S. Capitol in Washington, D.C., remains as the seat of Indiana's government, serving as home to the house of representatives, senate, supreme court, court of appeals, and a host of state agencies. Thanks to an approximately $11 million restoration project completed in time for the building's 1988 centennial, today's Hoosiers can walk through its skylighted, marble-topped corridors and marvel at the structure's classic features.

Of course, as with many government-sponsored projects, erecting such a stately edifice took plenty of time and generated a great deal of paperwork. Overseeing the building of the new statehouse in 1877 was the five-member Board of State House Commissioners, which consisted of the governor and two members of each political party. The commission engaged the services of an architect, civil engineer, and builder to examine four designs for the new capitol that had been received by the state prior to March 1877. They were to judge if these designs could be completed according to plans and specifications within the $2 million limit, whether dangers from fire were sufficiently guarded against, if ample provisions were made for safely heating the building, and if the materials of the superstructure were "in kind and quality such as to insure stability and permanence." All of the plans were rejected for not meeting the requirements imposed by the commissioners. As well as ridding itself of old plans, the board had to clean its own house, firing its secretary, W. C. Tarkington, in January 1878 because he was attempting to influence the selection of a design for which he would receive money.

In hopes of improving its decision-making ability, the commission visited Springfield, Peoria, and Chicago, Illinois;

Hartford, Connecticut; Lansing, Michigan; Washington, D.C.; and Cincinnati, Ohio, to examine the public buildings in these locales. Thus armed, the commissioners held an open competition for the statehouse design and received twenty-four plans. On 11 April 1878 the board accepted the design submitted by May, a Boston native who had come to Indiana in 1840 and was known for his work on the Northern Indiana Prison at Michigan City and county courthouses in Allen, Decatur, Hamilton, and Knox Counties. May called his plans for the capitol "Lucidus Ordo," Latin for "a clear arrangement." As his fee, May received 2 percent of the building's cost.

Although the project was delayed for a bit due to lawsuits brought by architects whose designs failed to win the competition, construction bids were finally opened by the commissioners on 15 August 1878. The contract was awarded to Kanmacher and Denig of Chicago, and work began on the new building that fall. The cornerstone, a ten-ton block of Indiana limestone inscribed with "A.D. 1880," was laid in ceremonies on 28 September 1880. Along with a keynote address by Gov. Thomas Hendricks, Indiana poet Sarah Bolton read a piece she had written for the occasion. The public took such a keen interest in the project that there were a number of accidents at the site, as well as incidents of people damaging materials and interfering with work. To halt the problems, the board ordered the statehouse grounds closed to the public.

A bigger problem had occurred in February 1880 when May, who was in Jacksonville, Florida, recuperating from an illness, died. In an attempt to keep the project running smoothly the board appointed Adolph Scherrer, who had been working by May's side for the past seven years, as supervising architect for the new statehouse. The commissioners also had to find a new contractor when in 1883 Kanmacher and Denig had trouble with its Chicago financier. New bids were solicited for the

building, and the board awarded the contract to Elias F. Gobel and Columbus Cummings of Chicago. The Indiana General Assembly held its first session in the new statehouse on 6 January 1887, but work continued at the site until September 1888. The Board of State House Commissioners concluded its work and closed its accounts on 2 October 1888.

Through the years the statehouse underwent extensive renovations to bring it up to modern conditions. During that time much of the building's original character was lost. In 1986 the legislature approved funding to return the statehouse to its 1888 appearance in time for the structure's centennial. The restoration, under the direction of Indianapolis's Cooler Group,

Inc., included stripping, painting, and decorating with the original 1886 designs approximately four acres of plaster walls and ceilings; using approximately 1,500 gallons of paint to re-create the original plans and refinish the area above the rotunda; cleaning approximately 124,500 square feet of interior marble and limestone; and removing 2,920 two-feet square pieces of marble floor so that new electrical wiring could be installed.

The results of the 1988 restoration can be viewed by taking a self-guided tour of the building, which is located at 200 W. Washington St., Indianapolis. Group tours can be arranged by calling the tour office at (317) 233-5293.

During the 1844 presidential campaign pitting Whig Henry Clay against Democrat James K. Polk, an Illinois attorney journeyed back to his Hoosier hometown to rally support for the Whig cause. After a long day of speechifying, the attorney retired for the night at the Gentryville home of his former employer, storekeeper William Jones.

Another guest at the Jones house that night, Nat Grigsby, recalled that during the night he and the attorney were awakened by a kitten. Grigsby said his Illinois friend "got up in the dark and said: 'Kitty, Kitty, Pussy, Pussy.' The cat knew the voice and manner kind. . . .[The visitor] took up the cat, carried it to the door, and gently rubbed it again and again . . . then gently put it down, closed the door, commenced telling stories and talking over old times."

The Illinois attorney who revisited his Indiana roots and partook of Jones's hospitality was Abraham Lincoln. Jones played an important role during Lincoln's fourteen-year residence in the state, employing him as a clerk and discussing the political issues of the time with him. Paradoxically, the two men changed places later in life, as Jones served his commander in chief as a colonel in the 53rd Regiment, Indiana Volunteers, during the Civil War.

Jones's important role in the early history of the nineteenth state is preserved by the Indiana State Museum System, which has made the Col. William Jones house in Gentryville a state historic site. The Spencer County attraction was placed on the National Register of Historic Places in 1975. Beginning in June 1976 the home underwent careful restoration to preserve its original Federal design.

Jones was born in Vincennes, Indiana, around 1800. His father, Peter Jones, operated the first hotel in that town. As a youth, according to an *Evansville Journal* article, Jones and several of his school friends were on hand to see the 1810 meeting between Indiana territorial governor William Henry Harrison and Shawnee warrior Tecumseh. About 1820 Jones moved to Louisville, where he clerked in a dry goods store. After suffering the loss of his wife and two children, Jones settled in Gentryville, Spencer County, in 1828.

Back in his native state, Jones worked as a clerk in a store owned by Gideon Romine. After a short time, however, Jones started a store of his own. Along with his new business, he took a new wife, marrying Rachel Oskin in April 1830. The couple had five sons—James, William, Henry Clay, Winfield Scott, and Charles. Two other children were killed when a keg of gunpowder accidentally exploded.

The Joneses first lived in a log home located on the south side of a road that passed through their farm, with their store on the opposite side of the road. A success in business, Jones built a new home (the present brick house) next to his store about 1834. Other families followed, and soon nearly a dozen cabins were established near the store. The little community was called Jonesboro.

Along with his business venture, Jones also served the area as a government official. He was elected county commissioner in 1833 and was postmaster for a number of years. Running on the Whig ticket, he served three terms (1838–41) as state representative. Although he sold his store in 1835 to his former employer, Romine, Jones returned to the merchant trade a year later in partnership with Joseph C. Richardson.

During his early years as a merchant in Spencer County, Jones has been credited by some as sometimes employing as a clerk in his store a gangling youth by the name of Abraham Lincoln. J. Edward Murr, in writing about Lincoln's life in the Hoosier State for the *Indiana Magazine of History*, said that Lincoln "drove a team for Jones, packed and unpacked boxes of goods, butchered and salted pork and at certain times performed some of the more menial services in the store proper such as the transfer of heavy and

cumbersome wares from the cellar to the main floor." Along with supplying the young Lincoln with employment, Jones also offered the future president a glimpse into the political happenings outside the Hoosier State through subscriptions to such newspapers as the *Louisville Journal*, which Lincoln read with great interest.

Jones was a Lincoln admirer throughout his life, vocally campaigning on Lincoln's behalf in his successful run for the White House in 1860. Jones's friendship with the new president, however, did not, as he and fellow Hoosier Grigsby hoped, translate into a federal job. The two men journeyed to Washington, D.C., met President Lincoln at the White House, and were warmly greeted and ushered into a room to meet Lincoln's wife, Mary. After introductions were made, and before the two men could stake their office claims, Lincoln told his wife: "Mary, you know I'm pestered and bothered continually by people coming here on the score of old acquaintance, as almost all of them have an ax to grind. They go on the theory that I've got offices to dispense with so numerous that I can give each one of them a place. Now here are two friends that have come to pay me a visit just because they are my friends, and haven't come to ask for any office or place. It is a relief to have this experience."

Even with that setback, Jones served his country, but on a different front. In December 1861, Indiana governor Oliver P. Morton commissioned Jones as a lieutenant colonel of volunteers. Jones

returned home and scoured Spencer, Perry, and Warrick Counties to find recruits for the 62nd Regiment, Indiana Volunteers, which was consolidated with the 53rd Regiment on 26 February 1862. Jones and the 53rd Regiment participated in the siege of Vicksburg, Mississippi, with Maj. Gen. Ulysses S. Grant's army, the attack on Meridian, Mississippi, with Maj. Gen. William T. Sherman's army, and Sherman's assault upon Confederate positions at Kennesaw Mountain, Georgia.

In July 1864 the 53rd Regiment was part of the Union force attempting to wrest Atlanta from Rebel troops. Before the battle, a

general advised the sixty-five-year-old Jones to resign his command and return home. An *Evansville Journal* article quoted him as replying, "I shall not resign, nor shall I go home until the last gun has been fired, the rebellion put down, and my country saved."

A few days later, on 22 July, Jones was leading his regiment when he was shot in both thighs. Col. Benjamin F. Potts of the 32nd Ohio Infantry reported that after the "brave and patriotic" Lieutenant Colonel Jones was first wounded, "he drew his revolver and assisted in guarding prisoners behind the works, where he received his death wound." A Confederate cannonball decapitated Jones. He was buried in Marietta National Cemetery in Georgia.

Following Jones's death, his home had a number of owners until 1887, when it was purchased by George and Arietta Seward Bullock, whose heirs owned the property until 1976. In 1976 William and Gayle Cook bought the crumbling home. Restoration began in June of that year by Pritchett Brothers Contractors of Springville, Indiana, who carefully numbered, dismantled, and reassembled every part of the house.

The Colonel William Jones State Historic Site is located on Old Boonville-Corydon Road, seven-tenths of a mile west of Highway 231, in Gentryville. The house is open from 9:00 A.M. to 5:00 P.M. Wednesday through Saturday and 1:00 P.M. to 5:00 P.M. on Sunday. The site is closed to the public from mid-December to mid-March. For more information, write the site at R.R. 1 Box 60D, Gentryville, IN 47537; or call (812) 937-2802.

Early in the nineteenth century, residents of Eaton, Ohio, could often be found shopping for the goods they needed at a general store owned by Cornelius Van Ausdall, a Dutch immigrant. Those who perused the store's collection of cotton goods, buttons, hardware, and other items were helped by a young clerk who had moved to the state in 1807 after his family had lost title to its land in Kentucky. Reminiscing about his days in the retail trade, the former clerk pointed to it as one of the most valuable periods in his life. "It taught me," he said, "to be industrious, active, methodical, and the value . . . of small things. I was brought into contact with all varieties of people, had to turn my hand to every kind of work, and learned how to be respectful and obliging to all."

The young clerk, James Franklin Doughty Lanier, learned his business lessons well. In his illustrious career, he served as clerk of the Indiana house of representatives, president of the Madison branch of the Indiana State Bank, promoter of the Madison and Indianapolis Railroad, cofounder of the Wall Street firm of Winslow, Lanier and Company, and financial savior of the Hoosier State during the Civil War. Lanier, who moved to Madison, Indiana, when it was a small community numbering only 150 citizens, became such a success that he was able to construct for himself and his family an impressive Greek Revival mansion with two-story columns and portico facing the Ohio River. Designed by noted architect Francis Costigan and completed in 1844, the home is now the Lanier Mansion State Historic Site and reflects the growth of Madison as a leading industrial and financial center for Indiana during its early years of statehood.

J. F. D. Lanier was born on 22 November 1800 in Washington, North Carolina. Soon after his birth Lanier and his family moved to Bourbon County, Kentucky. Lanier's father, Alexander Chalmers Lanier, invested in property there but lost title to his land and was forced to move his family to Eaton, Ohio. While in Ohio, Alexander Lanier worked as clerk of the county courts and subsequently served as an officer under William Henry Harrison during the War of 1812. In 1817 the Lanier family moved to Madison, Indiana, where the senior Lanier operated a dry goods store. Looking back on his early days in the Hoosier State, J. F. D. Lanier, in his autobiography (printed privately for family members), recalled that the community was "wholly without streets, or any improvements fitted to make it an attractive or agreeable place." Helping his father in the family's store whenever he was not attending school, Lanier received an appointment to West Point through his father's friendship with Harrison. He turned it down, however, because his mother, Drusilla Doughty Lanier, appeared to be "greatly distressed at the thought of my leaving home, I being her only child."

Instead of a military career, Lanier turned to the field of law for his livelihood. After studying in the office of Alexander A. Meek, a Madison attorney, Lanier received further training at the Transylvania Law School. Opening a practice back home in Madison, Lanier embarked on what proved to be a successful career. Traveling by horseback throughout southeastern Indiana to ply his trade, Lanier strove in his work "to be respected, and made it a point to be punctual in every duty and appointment. It was early my purpose of life to respect scrupulously the rights of others, but always to be firm in the assertion of my own." For Lanier, however, the "labor and anxiety" associated with his law practice proved to be too much for his strength, and he turned to politics.

In 1824 Lanier received an appointment as assistant clerk of the Indiana house of representatives, then meeting in Corydon. Three years later he became the house's chief clerk and received $3.50 per day for his labors. His service in the legislature became, according to Lanier, one of the chief causes of his future success. "It enabled me to form an intimate acquaintance with all

the leading men of the State, many of whom, in after life," he said, "were not slow to reciprocate the good offices I had done them." When the Second State Bank of Indiana was chartered in 1834, Lanier, who also dabbled in real estate, became president of the bank's Madison branch and a member of the board of control for the state system.

Lanier's business acumen was tested in 1837 when a severe financial panic swept the nation, leaving numerous banks in ruin. In spite of its relative youth, the Indiana State Bank weathered the financial crisis. Old Northwest historian R. Carlyle Buley noted that the bank's record "stands out in contrast with most of the flimsy banks of the day." Lanier proudly pointed out in his autobiography that the Indiana financial institution "not only paid dividends . . . but returned to its stockholders nearly double the original investment when it was wound up at the expiration of its charter in 1854." Lanier had a

direct hand in keeping the Indiana bank on solid footing. When the financial crisis broke, the bank had $1,500,000 in government funds on deposit. Board of control members called upon fellow member Lanier to travel to Washington, D.C., to confer with Secretary of the Treasury Levi Woodbury on what to do during this emergency. On his trip Lanier took with him $80,000 in gold. "I suffered not a little anxiety," he later admitted, "on account of the treasure I carried more than 300 miles through a wild and comparatively uninhabited region." Reaching the nation's capital safely, Lanier met with Woodbury and delivered the gold to him. "He received me with great cordiality," said Lanier, "and said that our bank was the *only one* that had offered to pay any portion of its indebtedness in specie."

With his financial success assured, Lanier embarked in 1840 on building for his family (he had married Elizabeth Gardner in 1819) a new home in Madison. The home, which took four years to build, attracted glowing reviews from the start of its construction. On 9 December 1843 the *Madison Courier* reported that "many gentlemen both from Cincinnati and Louisville, who have been in our place and examined this building, have said that in point of architectural beauty and workmanship, it surpasses any thing in those cities; and several gentlemen from eastern cities have also acknowledged that they have seen nothing there superior to it." Lanier lived in his new home for only a few years. His wife, Elizabeth, died from tuberculosis in 1846, and two years later Lanier married Mary McClure of Carlisle, Pennsylvania. In 1851 the couple moved to New York City, where two years earli-

er Lanier had formed a partnership with Richard H. Winslow, a Wall Street businessman. The firm, Winslow, Lanier and Company, had as its chief business, according to Lanier, "the negotiation of railway securities, although we contemplated, in connection therewith, a general banking business."

Removed from Indiana, Lanier nevertheless continued to play an important role in the nineteenth state's affairs. With the outbreak of the Civil War, Indiana governor Oliver P. Morton had telegraphed President Abraham Lincoln to pledge the raising of ten thousand men for the Union army. The state, however, had no money in its

treasury to equip the new troops. Governor Morton turned to Lanier for help, and the businessman responded with funds that eventually totaled $420,000. Morton again turned to Lanier for aid in 1863 when a divided legislature collapsed in mutual recriminations (Democrats had attempted to reduce the governor's control over the state militia, causing the Republicans to abandon the session) and failed to pass needed appropriations for the state government's operation. "The application [for assistance] was made at the darkest period of the whole war," Lanier said. "I could have no security whatever, and could rely for reimbursement only on the good faith of a Legislature to be chosen at a future and distant day." In spite of these difficulties, Lanier agreed to help Morton, reasoning that if he refused financial assistance it might start a domino effect that would render it impossible for the federal government "to sustain the immense burdens of the war." Lanier's loans to the state during this crisis reached $640,000, an amount Indiana managed to pay back to its benefactor over the years.

While Lanier lived in New York until his death on 27 August 1881, the family's children retained ownership of the mansion back in Madison. Alexander C. Lanier, the businessman's eldest son, lived in the home from 1851 until his death in 1895. A Yale University graduate, Alexander, who received title to the property from his father in 1861 "in consideration of natural love and affection, and of one dollar," gained a well-deserved reputation as an amateur horticulturist by maintaining and improving the mansion's gardens and greenhouses. Blanche Goode Garber, a Madison resident, described the garden: "Here dwarf fruit trees of choicest varieties, berries and good things less poetic abounded; wire frames draped with varicolored sweet-peas screened the homelier but more necessary food patches; holly, red with berries in their season, hydrangeas, wisterias, clematis, syringas and spireas, flowers of each season in its turn, kept a ceaseless successing of bloom."

Upon Alexander Lanier's death, the house became the property of his widow, Stella. Family members occupied the home until the early 1900s, when it was given to the Jefferson County Historical Society. In 1925 the Lanier family turned the mansion over to the State of Indiana as its first state memorial (now a state historic site). The three-story, eighteen-room mansion, complete with a spiral staircase, has undergone several restorations over the years. In 1990 the state decided to restore the house and grounds to the period of its first occupant, J. F. D. Lanier, and architect, Francis Costigan. The site conducted six years of intensive research into the family, gardens, and structure, concentrating on the period 1844 to 1851. Using money donated by private individuals, groups, and foundations, the site used nationally renowned experts for every area (lighting, paint analysis, curtains and carpets, and so on) of the research and restoration. Today the Lanier Mansion is one of the best places in the nation to see what life was like in an 1840s city estate.

The entire 134-city-block area of downtown Madison has been recognized for its nationally significant architecture and history by being placed on the National Register of Historic Places. The Lanier Mansion, a National Historic Landmark, is open from 9:00 A.M. to 5:00 P.M. Tuesday through Saturday and from 1:00 P.M. to 5:00 P.M. on Sunday. The site is closed to the public from mid-December to mid-March. For more information, write the site at 511 W. First St., Madison, IN 47250; or call (812) 265-3526.

Richard Flower, an Englishman traveling to a settlement of his fellow country-men in the Illinois Territory in 1819, came across an intriguing town on his jour-ney. Writing to a friend back in Great Britain, Flower noted that he spent a week "at Harmony, that wonder of the West," located along the Wabash River in the young state of Indiana. He wrote that the community, a group of Lutheran Separatists led by George Rapp, was well worth visiting. The Harmonists, as the group was known, immigrated to America in 1804 from Württemberg, Germany, and founded a communal society in Butler County, Pennsylvania, bound togeth-er by a belief in the imminent Second Coming of Christ, obedience to their leader Rapp, and celibacy. After moving to southwestern Indiana in 1814, the group built a thriving, self-sufficient community where, as Flower noted, "perfect equality prevails, and there are not servants; but plenty of persons who serve. Every man has his station appointed him according to his ability, and every one has his wants supplied according to his wishes."

Although the Harmony Society found success in the Hoosier State, a need to be closer to eastern markets, as well as troubles with its neighbors, forced the society to sell its property to Welsh-born industrialist Robert Owen in 1825. Owen, who hoped to introduce an enlightened social system to America, brought with him to New Harmony (the new name for the community) such eminent people as geologist and philanthropist William Maclure, naturalists Thomas Say and Charles-Alexandre Lesueur, and educators Joseph Neef, Phiquepal d'Arusmont, and Marie Duclos Fretageot. Owen's utopian dream never came to fruition, but his attempt did have an impact on American science and education. The story of these two nineteenth-century communal societies is spread through the work of Historic New Harmony, a unified program of the University of Southern Indiana and the Indiana State Museum and Historic Sites.

Johann Georg Rapp, the leader of the utopian community called by historian Karl Arndt "the socio-economic showplace of America in the first half of the nineteenth century," was born in the small village of Iptingen in Württemberg on 1 November 1757. From an early age, Rapp displayed leadership ability. Arndt noted that when Rapp's parents sent him on an errand to gather grass growing along the roadside, he persuaded his schoolmates to do his chore for him while "he climbed up a convenient tree to edify them with his preaching." At first a weaver by trade, Rapp eventually attracted a band of devoted followers—the Harmony Society—who believed they were God's chosen people, abandoning private property for communal living. Searching for religious freedom, Rapp and his retinue left their native country for the United States in 1803. They settled in Pennsylvania.

Seeking a better climate and room to expand their growing society, the Harmonists sold their settlement in Pennsylvania in 1814 and moved their community, which numbered between seven hundred and eight hundred, to the approximately twenty-five thousand acres of land they had bought along the Wabash

River in today's Posey County, Indiana. Writing to his adopted son Frederick in November 1815, Rapp noted that the area intended for their settlement included "plenty of pasture for sheep on high land, watered by beautiful fresh brooks, and as long as we live here we will not have to lift our feet over a stone, and fields and meadows are as level as living room floors."

During the ten years the Harmonists lived in the nineteenth state they created a thriving, prosperous community, called by one historian the "most successful economic enterprise in Indiana." By 1819 the community included 150 log houses, 9 stables, 24 corncribs, a shoe and tailor shop, 2 sawmills, a woolen factory, a blacksmith shop, a wagonmaker's shop, a carpenter's shop, and a number of other ventures. To support the community the Harmonists sold a variety of agricultural and other products, including: wheat, corn, oats, sugar, tobacco, cheese, hops, hemp, rye, barley, pork, venison, eggs, bacon, honey, wool, flax, cider, apples, and grass seed. These products, noted Arndt, were sold to markets from Pittsburgh to New Orleans.

In spite of the financial success enjoyed by the Harmony Society, market distribution and local difficulties forced Rapp to look for a buyer for the property. To sell the property, Rapp called upon Flower, who, although not a Harmonist himself, was very familiar with the community. Flower had a three-page advertisement for the settlement printed in London, which recommended the town as particularly suited for capitalists or "large Religious Communities who may be desirous to form a settlement." In 1825 Rapp sold the Harmonie settlement for approximately $150,000 to Owen, who dubbed the area New Harmony. The Harmony Society moved to Economy, Pennsylvania, where, after disagreements broke out over the community's direction and numbers dwindled because of the practice of celibacy, the Harmonists gradually faded into history.

In his opening address at New Harmony on 27 April 1825,

OLD NO: 2
Rappite Community Building
Mens Dormitory-Built (1816-22)
Later Became the Workshop of
Owen Scientist and Home of
Joseph Neefs Pestalozzian
School
~ In 1826 ~

Owen stated that he had come to the United States to "introduce an entire new State of society; to change it from the ignorant, selfish system, to an enlightened social system, which shall gradually unite all interests into one, and remove all cause for contest between individuals." All members of the community shared equally in labor and the fruits of that labor. A constitution for a Preliminary Society, which received approval in May 1825, provided for membership open to people "of all ages and descriptions," except for "persons of color." Before the end of the year, the community's population had grown to one thousand people. In January 1826 the keelboat *Philanthropist*, later known as the Boatload of Knowledge and headed by Maclure, docked at New Harmony and unloaded scientists and teachers for the new community.

Just two years after the social experiment began, Owen gave up on his dream and returned to Scotland; his community had been an economic failure. New Harmony had, however, contributed greatly to American society. Its residents had established in Indiana the first free library, a public school system open to males and females, and a civic dramatic club, and the town had served as the second headquarters of the U.S. Geological Survey. Also, Owen's sons—Robert Dale Owen and David Dale Owen—remained in Indiana to continue the New Harmony tradition of reformist leadership. Robert Dale Owen served as an Indiana congressman and sponsored legislation establishing the Smithsonian Institution, while David Dale Owen worked as Indiana State Geologist and later as a geologist for the federal government. Both brothers were involved heavily in the Smithsonian's planning, design, and construction.

Over the years New Harmony changed, but subsequent generations preserved the area's communal past. In 1937 the state created the first New Harmony Commission to help purchase and preserve key historic properties. In 1959 the Robert Lee Blaffer Trust, founded by Jane Blaffer Owen, initiated the first in a series of several contemporary additions to New Harmony, including the Roofless Church and the New Harmony Inn. The state restored Community House #2, formerly a residence for single Harmonists, and rescued Community House #4 and returned it to its 1888 appearance as Thrall's Opera House. Growth continued in the years to come as Historic New Harmony, Inc. (created in 1974 to carry out a comprehensive restoration plan) selected Richard Meier to design the Atheneum/Visitors Center, which opened in 1979. Today Historic New Harmony offers visitors tours of historic properties, special events, theatrical performances, and contemporary art exhibitions.

Tours for Historic New Harmony begin at the Atheneum/Visitors Center, two blocks north of Highway 66 on Arthur and North Streets in New Harmony. Group tours are offered year-round. For more information, write Historic New Harmony at P.O. Box 579, New Harmony, IN 47631; or call (800) 231-2168.

Growing up in the east-central Indiana community of Muncie at the turn of the twentieth century, Hoosier author Emily Kimbrough experienced a happy childhood in a town where she "was not a stranger to anyone." Contributing to her happiness were the times she enjoyed with her best friend Betty, who lived in a house situated along the banks of the White River on Minnetrista Boulevard. During the spring the two friends explored the scenic grounds of Betty's home and prepared "magic concoctions from leaves and grass and acorns, and one or two secret ingredients," Kimbrough recalled in her book *How Dear to My Heart*. "Then we would fill little candy boxes, which we had collected and saved all Winter, and tie them to trees all over Betty's place," she noted. These elaborate preparations were made in hopes of attracting fairies as visitors. "I hoped for them [fairies] with all my heart, but I doubted a little," said Kimbrough. "Betty had not the slightest doubt."

The place that inspired such magical thoughts was Oakhurst, a Victorian home built in 1895 as the residence of George Alexander and Frances Woodworth Ball.

Designed by Indianapolis architect Louis Gibson, the unique shingle-style structure was also the birthplace and home for the Balls' only child, Elisabeth, the Betty who Kimbrough remembered as a staunch believer in fantastic creatures. Oakhurst, where Elisabeth lived from her birth in 1897 until her death on 29 April 1982, served as her muse (she wrote numerous poems and sketches) and instilled in her a lifelong interest in botany and natural history. To mark Oakhurst's one hundredth anniversary, the Minnetrista Cultural Center in 1995, through funding by the George and Frances Ball Foundation, restored and renovated the former Ball residence and its six and a half acres—known as Oakhurst Gardens—in order to create an awareness, understanding, and appreciation of the natural environment.

Oakhurst is just one part of the legacy left by the five Ball brothers (Edmund, Frank, George, Lucius, and William) who were searching for new opportunities after the family's glass canning jar factory in Buffalo, New York, was destroyed in an 1886 fire. Drawn to Muncie because of the ready supply of natural gas, and the city's offer of seven acres of land and $5,000 to help offset moving expenses, the Ball brothers opened their factory in 1888. Twelve years later the firm became the country's largest producer of glass jars. With their business venture prospering, the Ball brothers turned their attention to constructing homes for their families. For advice they turned to their sister Lucina Ball, who wrote from Philadelphia in 1892 that they should "buy enough land for at least three houses or form a 'syndicate' and buy a block of town lots." She also reminded her brothers that their recently deceased mother, Maria Polly Bingham Ball, had always wanted the Ball family to both live and work together in harmony.

Taking his sister's advice to heart, in 1893 Frank C. Ball bought approximately thirty acres of land along the north bank of the White River just outside the Muncie city limits, distancing the Balls from the city's noise and grime. Trumpeting the purchase on its front pages, the *Muncie Daily Times* predicted that in a short time "this will be the prettiest place in or around Muncie from the fact that the Ball brothers will expend over $40,000 in making it a palace and garden." The newspaper also noted that a sixty-foot-wide boulevard was to be constructed fifty feet above the water's edge. Ball sisters Lucina and Frances devised a name for the site, Minnetrista, that combined the Native American word for water, *minne*, with the Middle English spelling of a word for an agreed upon meeting place, *trist*.

The first Ball brother to build a house on the site was Frank, who hired Indianapolis architect Gibson to design a nineteen-room frame residence, which was finished in 1895 (fire destroyed the home in 1967), in time for the birth of the

Balls' second child. Lucina Ball, who had suggested buying the property in the first place, may also have alerted the Ball brothers about Gibson's talent as a home designer. In an 18 March 1894 letter to George Ball and his new wife, Frances, Lucina, discussing the trials and tribulations in finding the right home, noted that the "Indianapolis architect, Gibson, seems from his book [*Convenient Houses*, published in 1889] to be a practical man. If you are not already settled on a plan, see him."

An Aurora, Indiana, native and an 1874 graduate of the Massachusetts Institute of Technology, Gibson, a friend of noted Chicago architect Louis Sullivan, had definite ideas about his art. "Money," he wrote in his 1895 book *Beautiful Houses*, "gives many people an opportunity to display bad taste. Houses are more frequently ruined by spending too much money than they are through not using enough." In building a house, an architect, according to Gibson, engaged in "a great character study" of his client in order to devise the proper design. "It would be altogether inconsistent and uncalled-for if the architect should insist upon clothing all his houses with the same character of design," he added.

Influenced by the shingle-style design through his schooling at MIT, work at a Boston architect's office, and more than a year's study in Europe, Gibson utilized it in preparing the second home on Minnetrista Boulevard: Oakhurst. "The mistake in the use of shingles has been in placing them where they do not belong," Gibson claimed. A shingle house, he insisted, should be associated with "a green lawn, a little clump of bushes, old fashioned roses, hollyhocks, and other picturesque flowers." Gibson, who apparently committed suicide in an Indianapolis hotel in 1907, was guided to the perfect spot for the home by one of its intended occupants. "Mother was particularly fond of the beautiful oak grove at the west end of Minnetrista, and asked for our home to be built there," noted Elisabeth Ball.

At the time of its construction, Oakhurst totaled approximately

two acres and included a number of natural settings, formal gardens, and exotic plant life. In crafting the three-story residence, Gibson kept in mind the idea that "in this great grove a structure simple in outline and fine and carefully considered in detail, would be reposeful in its association with the picturesque surroundings."

After Oakhurst's completion, the other Ball brothers also built homes on the Minnetrista land. Instead of constructing a new home like his brothers, Dr. Lucius Ball purchased an existing farmhouse on the Minnetrista property. At the urging of Edmund Burke Ball, the building, which had faced Wheeling Avenue, was turned to face Minnetrista Boulevard. In 1897 William and Emma Ball moved into a red-brick house of Georgian design located just east of Oakhurst, which they dubbed Maplewood. At the turn of the century, a brick walk, which Elisabeth Ball called Aunt Emma's Walk, connected the two homes. In 1904 Edmund Ball hired Fort Wayne architect Marshall S. Mahurin, who worked on remodeling Frank Ball's house the previous year and also designed Muncie's Carnegie library, to plan a Gothic Revival-style residence.

Although different in design, the Ball brothers' homes were all filled with the same thing: the sounds of children. George and Frances Ball's only child, Elisabeth, was born on 26 December 1897. Elisabeth Ball fashioned a rich life for herself at Oakhurst, expanding on her mother's work of beautifying the grounds, writing poetry and tips on gardening, and collecting butterflies, artwork, and children's books (a hobby Elisabeth inherited from her father). Her childhood was idyllic.

From the first, Elisabeth Ball and Emily Kimbrough became, like their mothers, best friends. The young Elisabeth, better known as Betty or Bee to her friends and family, was small in stature with "blue eyes that were nearly always solemn and usually anxious," Kimbrough remembered. "Her hair was yellow and it was bobbed, with a bang across the front. The cut of her hair

closed in her face, making it more tiny." Even at an early age, Ball had a knack for weaving a convincing tale. Kimbrough recalled one incident when, while eating lunch at the future writer's East Washington Street home, Ball boldly announced to Kimbrough's mother: "I cannot eat any more spinach, because there is a fairy sitting on it." Kimbrough's mother failed in her repeated attempts to convince Ball to eat her spinach and finally gave up trying. "But if I said, 'I see a fairy, too, on mine,' Mother always answered me, 'Eat your spinach, Emily,'" Kimbrough wryly noted.

Following in her mother's footsteps, Elisabeth Ball attended Vassar College where, after first specializing in English and history, she switched her major to botany. After graduation, Ball, who never married, lived at Oakhurst and expanded and improved its grounds. During the 1930s as many as ten full-time gardeners worked to help her develop the natural setting at the home by planting thousands of flowers—daffodils, hyacinths, peonies, poppies, tulips, Virginia bluebells, and yellow buttercups—and other plants. "We have kept the natural setting. I have made studies of native plants and shrubs and wild flowers—have photographed them all in natural color," said Ball. "I have raised dogwood and redbud from seedlings that I got in our woods." Along with photographing the results of her efforts, Ball kept extensive notes and drawings about the different species planted each season.

Ball shared her gardening experiences with others through articles written for newspapers and horticultural magazines. In the 1930s she had a log cabin constructed on the property as a place where she could go and spend hours crafting her poetry, journal entries, and other literary endeavors.

After Elisabeth Ball's death at age eighty-four in 1982, Oakhurst remained empty until 1990, when the Minnetrista Cultural Foundation was deeded the property by the Ball Brothers Foundation and began an environmentally friendly restoration of the grounds, which had been allowed to revert to a wild state in Ball's last years, and home. A new cabin was built to serve as the site for presentations on nature and the environment. Oakhurst itself was renovated to its height-of-occupancy period, the era between the two world wars. The house's second floor is used as a changing exhibition space. The Lucius Ball home, which serves as an orientation center for Oakhurst and its gardens, also received restoration work. Offices and a library are located on the home's second floor.

Oakhurst Gardens is open from 10:00 A.M. to 5:00 P.M. Tuesday through Saturday and 1:00 P.M. to 5:00 P.M. on Sunday. For more information, write Oakhurst at 600 W. Minnetrista Blvd., Muncie, IN 47303; or call (765) 282-4848 or (800) 428-5887.

OLD LIGHTHOUSE MUSEUM

Michigan City

On 19 March 1861 the citizens of Michigan City learned that President Abraham Lincoln had decided to appoint a new keeper for what was then Indiana's only lighthouse on the Great Lakes. For an annual salary of $600, the new lighthouse keeper—a cousin of Schuyler Colfax, *St. Joseph Valley Register* editor and later vice president under Ulysses S. Grant—faced the arduous task of twice-nightly trips to recharge the lamp with lard oil. In forty-three years on the job, the keeper faithfully kept the beacon lit, earning the title of "the sailor's true friend." The keeper's name was Harriet A. Colfax.

The Old Lighthouse Museum, which is operated by the Michigan City Historical Society, preserves the memories of Harriet Colfax and others like her who helped guide sailors safely through the often dangerous waters of Lake Michigan. Although the lighthouse, which was placed on the National Register of Historic Places in 1974, is no longer in operation, it still manages to shed light on the history of the city and life on the lake.

Dubbed Old Faithful by grateful sailors, the lighthouse was established in 1835 when Maj. Isaac C. Elston, the original purchaser of the land on which Michigan City was founded, deeded to the federal government a strip of land running from the bend of Trail Creek to Lake Michigan for the construction of a lighthouse. The first light, however, was not in a building but was instead a postlight—a lantern on top of a tall post—located approximately one hundred feet west of the present lighthouse.

Constructing a permanent structure proved to be a challenge. Although a $7,000 contract was let in 1836 for a forty-foot-high whitewashed lighthouse tower topped with a lantern and a keeper's dwelling, the contractors had to endure such hardships as the loss of building materials in a storm and funding delays. Unfortunately, because funds originally appropriated for the work were not used in that fiscal year, the monies had to be returned to the government. The funds were reappropriated, however, and the lighthouse was finally completed in 1837.

One witness described the finished product as "a story and a half house, plastered on the outside and dazzling in its whiteness, more of a portico than a veranda ornamented the front and was covered with trailing vines. It fronted south and was surrounded by a grove of small oaks on the west. The well-kept lawn was dotted with shrubbery, flowers, and enclosed by a low rustic fence, and from a little wicket gate led a white graveled walk to the residence. The lighttower was a detached cone-shaped structure." The first lighthouse keeper, Edmund B. Harrison, was appointed on 9 December 1837 and received $350 per year for his efforts.

Twenty-one years after the lighthouse was completed, the federal government, spurred on by the need for a brighter light for the increased shipping traffic on the lake, built a new lighthouse using Joliet stone for the foundation and Milwaukee brick for the upper portion. The date of construction, 1858, was inscribed on the south wall. The lighthouse's north end contained a French-designed Fresnel lens, fueled by sperm whale oil, the light from which could be seen for fifteen miles.

A native of Ogdensburg, New York, Harriet Colfax came to Michigan City in 1853 reportedly to forget a failed romance. Before her appointment as lighthouse keeper, she worked as a typesetter for her brother, Richard Colfax, *Michigan City Gazette* publisher, and also gave music lessons. She was aided in her lighthouse duties by Ann Hartwell, who taught school in Michigan City. Although described as having a petite figure "peculiarly unfitted for the position of lightkeeper," Colfax faithfully kept the light burning despite often adverse conditions.

In 1871 a small postlight was installed on the east pier and later was moved to the west pier. Colfax had the responsibility of

keeping the beacon lighted, even though she had to cross Trail Creek by boat to service the light. Patricia Harris, former museum curator, described one particularly rough journey endured by Colfax: "Miss Colfax warmed the lard oil and started on her hazardous trip. Twice she was driven back before she gained the beacon, and when at last she reached it, she found to her dismay and annoyance that the lock had been tampered with and it would not open. In her desperation she finally broke a pane of glass, crawled through the opening and inserted the lamp in place. However, so much time had been lost that the oil had congealed and would not ignite. Lamp in hand, she started back to the lighthouse through an icy shower, slipped, fell, rose and slipped again, but finally reached the end of the pier in safety. The oil was again heated and again she started out for the beacon, this time accomplishing her task."

In addition to her usual chores as lighthouse keeper, Colfax dutifully kept journals that recorded such events as boat dockings, weather conditions, shipwrecks, and lighthouse conditions. In one entry Colfax noted that the lock of the beacon had been "tampered with by some parties who had not the fear of the law

before their eyes." Her last entry, upon her retirement in October 1904, read: "Fair, warm wind, smokey atmosphere. Received another call from Mr. [Thomas] Armstrong, my successor." She died five months later at the age of eighty.

The federal government extensively renovated the lighthouse in 1904 by adding two rooms to each floor on the north side and creating duplex apartments. Workmen also removed the tower from the roof. The keeper and his family used all three floors on the east side, and the assistant keeper used those on the west. On 20 October 1904 the lantern was moved to a new fog-signal lighthouse at the entrance of Michigan City's harbor.

In 1933 the light in the harbor was electrified, and the keeper on shore could turn it on by simply flipping a switch. Six years later the U.S. Coast Guard assumed responsibility for the light. Since the Coast Guard had its own station a short distance from the old lighthouse, it rented the structure as a private residence for a time; the building also served as home to the Coast Guard Auxiliary. The lighthouse gradually deteriorated before the government declared it surplus property in 1960.

The Government Services Administration sold the old

lighthouse to the city in 1963 for $18,500. Two years later the Michigan City Historical Society entered into a lease with the city to restore the facility and turn it into a museum within two years. However, it took eight years and approximately $100,000 to renovate the property. On 9 June 1973 the Old Lighthouse Museum was officially dedicated and opened to the public.

The Old Lighthouse Museum features photographs and memorabilia relating to the lighthouse's operation and those who worked there. The museum also features items on the history of Michigan City, shipwreck artifacts, and many other items. One of the unique stories told by the museum is that of inventor Lodner Darvontis Phillips, who launched the first submarine to sail on the Great Lakes from the foot of the old lighthouse in 1851.

The Old Lighthouse Museum is located on Heisman Harbor Road in Michigan City's Washington Park. The museum is open from 1:00 P.M. to 4:00 P.M. Tuesday through Sunday. For more information, write the Old Lighthouse Museum at P.O. Box 512, Michigan City, IN 46361; or call (219) 872-6133.

ERNIE PYLE STATE HISTORIC SITE

Dana

The American campaign against the Japanese on Okinawa still raged when a war correspondent new to the Pacific theater stepped ashore on Ie Shima, a small island just west of Okinawa. Traveling with a group of infantrymen, the reporter was killed by Japanese machine-gun fire. Saddened by their loss, the soldiers paid tribute to their fallen friend with a simple plaque that read: "At this spot, the 77th Infantry Division lost a buddy, Ernie Pyle, 18 April 1945."

To the millions of people on the American home front during World War II, Ernie Pyle's column offered a foxhole view of the struggle as he reported on the life, and sometimes death, of the average soldier. When he died, Pyle's readership was worldwide, with his column appearing in four hundred daily and three hundred weekly newspapers. Nobel Prize–winning author John Steinbeck, a Pyle friend, perhaps summed up the reporter's work best when he told a *Time* magazine reporter: "There are really two wars and they haven't much to do with each other. There is the war of maps and logistics, of campaigns, of ballistics, armies, divisions and regiments—and that is General [George] Marshall's war. Then there is the war of homesick, weary, funny, violent, common men who wash their socks in their helmets, complain about the food, whistle at the Arab girls, or any girls for that matter, and lug themselves through as dirty a business as the world has ever seen and do it with humor and dignity and courage—and that is Ernie Pyle's war."

Pyle's legacy is maintained in the Hoosier State by the Ernie Pyle State Historic Site in Dana. The Vermillion County site preserves Pyle's restored birthplace. The building was moved from its original farm location to Dana in 1976 through the efforts of the Indiana Department of the American Legion.

Ernest Taylor Pyle was born on 3 August 1900 on the Sam Elder farm, located south and west of Dana, where his father was a tenant farmer. Pyle, the only child of Will and Maria Pyle, disliked farming, once noting that "anything was better than looking at the south end of a horse going north." After his high school graduation, Pyle—caught up in the patriotic fever sweeping the nation upon America's entry into World War I—enlisted in the Naval Reserve. Before he could complete his training, however, an armistice was declared in Europe.

In 1919 Pyle enrolled at Indiana University in Bloomington. He left the university in 1923, just short of finishing a degree in journalism, to accept a reporter's job at the *La Porte Herald*. A few months later, lured by an offer of an extra $2.50 per week, Pyle joined the staff of the *Washington (D.C.) Daily News*, part of the Scripps-Howard newspaper chain.

On 25 July 1925 Pyle married Minnesota native Geraldine Siebolds. By 1926 the Pyles had quit their jobs to barnstorm around the country, traveling nine thousand miles in just ten

weeks. Pyle returned to the *Washington Daily News* in 1927 and began the country's first-ever daily aviation column. He was the newspaper's managing editor for three years before becoming a roving columnist for Scripps-Howard. In the next five years he crossed the continent some thirty-five times. Columns from this period were compiled in the book *Home Country*.

Pyle journeyed to England in 1940 to report on the Battle of Britain. Witnessing a German firebombing raid on London, he wrote that it was "the most hateful, most beautiful single scene I have ever known." A book of his experiences during this time, *Ernie Pyle in England*, was published in 1941. A year later he began covering America's involvement in the war, reporting on Allied operations in North Africa, Sicily, Italy, and France. The columns he wrote based on his experiences during these campaigns are contained in the books *Here Is Your War* and *Brave Men*.

Although Pyle's columns covered almost every branch of the service—from quartermaster troops to pilots—he saved his highest praise and devotion for the common foot soldier. "I love the infantry because they are the underdogs," he wrote. "They are the mud-rain-frost-and-wind boys. They have no comforts, and they even learn to live without the necessities. And in the end they are the guys that wars can't be won without."

The Hoosier reporter's columns not only described the soldier's hardships but also spoke out on his behalf. In a column from Italy in 1944, Pyle proposed that combat soldiers be given "fight pay," similar to an airman's flight pay. In May of that year Congress acted on Pyle's suggestion, giving soldiers 50 percent extra pay for combat service, legislation nicknamed the Ernie Pyle Bill.

Despite the warmth he felt for the average GI, Pyle had no illusions about the dangers involved with his own job. He once wrote a friend that he tried "not to take any foolish chances, but there's just no way to play it completely safe and still do your job."

Weary from his work in Europe, Pyle grudgingly accepted

what was to be his last assignment, covering the action in the Pacific with the navy and marines. He rationalized his acceptance, noting, "What can a guy do? I know millions of others who are reluctant too, and they can't even get home."

After Pyle's tragic death, Edwin Waltz, the reporter's personal secretary at Pacific Fleet headquarters in Guam, went through his personal effects and discovered a draft of a column Pyle had handwritten in anticipation of the war's end in Europe. In that column, which was never published, Pyle wrote that he would not soon forget "the unnatural sight of cold dead men scattered over the hillsides and in the ditches along the high rows of hedge throughout the world.

"Dead men by mass production—in one country after another—month after month and year after year. Dead men in winter and dead men in summer.

"Dead men in such familiar promiscuity that they become monotonous.

"Dead men in such monstrous infinity that you come almost to hate them."

Hoosiers can gain insight into the life and writings of America's most famed war correspondent by visiting his childhood home in Dana. At one time Pyle's home was in danger of being obliterated from the Indiana landscape. In 1973 a fundraising campaign was started to raise $110,000 for restoring the house. The two-story white farmhouse was opened to the public as a state memorial in 1976 as part of the bicentennial celebration.

Pyle lived in the farmhouse for the first eighteen months of his young life. The home's living room, bedroom, and kitchen include original pieces from the Pyle household. Also on display are items from Pyle's newspaper career: his canteen, his dufflebag, the jacket he wore to tea with Eleanor Roosevelt, and the telegram informing his parents of their son's death. The site also features a visitors center, built using two World War II–era Quonset huts. The center includes a video theater, a library, exhibitions, and a gift shop.

The Ernie Pyle State Historic Site, part of the Indiana State Museum System, is located on Highway 71 in downtown Dana, just one mile north of Highway 36. The site is open from 9:00 A.M. to 5:00 P.M. Tuesday through Saturday and 1:00 P.M. to 5:00 P.M. Sunday. The site is closed mid-December through mid-March. For more information, write the Ernie Pyle State Historic Site at P.O. Box 338, Dana, IN 47847; or call (765) 665-3633.

An Indianapolis poet who had recently begun to garner attention for his work in the *Indianapolis Journal* was out driving with a friend in the city one afternoon in 1880 when he came upon a shady spot at the corner of Lockerbie and East Streets. While taking in the sights, the onetime traveling sign painter chanced to see a young lady drive past in a small, clay-colored carriage, stop, and enter a stately brick home. Entranced by what he had seen, the Hoosier writer returned to the area a few days later. "Walking back to the office, I repeated the phrase with every footstep— Lockerbie Street—Lockerbie Street. The words clung to me like tickseed to a tiger," he said. From the experience he wrote the poem "Lockerbie Street," which was published in the *Journal*. The work lauded the thoroughfare for offering relief "from the clangor and din" of the big city and offering "sheltering shade" to those who wandered its path. The day the poem appeared, the poet discovered that his office had been stuffed full of flowers from grateful Lockerbie Street residents.

The bard in question, James Whitcomb Riley, had numerous opportunities to experience the pleasures of residing in such quiet and contemplative surroundings.

From the summer of 1893 until his death in 1916, Riley lived at 528 Lockerbie Street as the paying guest in Maj. Charles L. Holstein's home, a two-story Italianate structure built in 1872 by Indianapolis baker John Nickum, Holstein's father-in-law and a Riley confidant. The house that sheltered the Hoosier poet for twenty-three years has, since 1922, been preserved as a historic site by the nonprofit James Whitcomb Riley Memorial Association. In addition to the Indianapolis site, Riley's boyhood home in Greenfield is maintained as the James Whitcomb Riley Birthplace and Boyhood Home, which serves as an interpretation center for the period of Riley's life following the family's move from the house.

Born in a two-room log cabin on 7 October 1849 in Greenfield, Riley was the second son and third of six children born to Reuben A.—a Civil War captain, lawyer, and Indiana legislator—and Elizabeth Marine Riley. With a successful law practice, Reuben Riley in 1850 moved his family from the log cabin to a home he helped design and build. As a child, Riley often accompanied his father (a noted political orator) on trips to the Hancock County courthouse, where he observed the manners and mores of country society, as well as the countrified dialect he later used in his poetry. He also became a frequent visitor to Brandywine Creek, located about a mile from the courthouse, a place he later memorialized as "The Old Swimmin'-Hole."

At an early age the future poet discovered that he disliked the "iron discipline" of school life but enjoyed books, music, and writing poetry. "My father did not encourage my verse making for he thought it too visionary, and being a visionary himself, he believed he understood the dangers of following the promptings of the poetic temperament," Riley said. "I doubted if anything would come of the verse writing myself." Leaving school at the age of sixteen, Riley attempted to read law in his father's office.

The Riley family fell on hard times following the Civil War. Reuben Riley's service in the Union army had caused him to lose some of his law clients, and when some land investments went sour he and his family were forced to leave their home and move to other quarters in Greenfield (James Whitcomb Riley bought back the old family home in 1893). Possessing a wanderlust spirit, the young Riley turned from the field of law to another pursuit—art. He traveled the countryside with a group of friends he dubbed "the Graphics" as a sign, house, and ornamental painter. Riley later became an advance agent for a traveling wagon show. In 1873 he returned to Greenfield and worked for the town's newspaper. A year earlier, his poetry, under the name Jay Whit, had first appeared in the *Indianapolis Saturday Mirror.*

After a short stint on the *Anderson Democrat*, where he was fired for perpetrating a hoax involving a supposed

long-lost Edgar Allan Poe poem, Riley found work on another newspaper, the *Indianapolis Journal*. While on the *Journal* staff Riley won acclaim for his poems, especially "When the Frost Is on the Punkin," part of a series he signed Benj. F. Johnson, of Boone. The series was published in book form in 1883 as *"The Old Swimmin'-Hole," and 'Leven More Poems*. Riley's characters— Old Aunt Mary, Little Orphant Annie, the Raggedy Man, Doc Sifers, and Uncle Sidney—along with his sentimental style, struck a chord with the reading public. Riley worked hard to spread his

fame, and help himself financially, through appearances on the lecture circuit with, among others, Edgar W. "Bill" Nye.

Riley's lectures helped make him a household name throughout the country, but his hectic schedule soon took its toll on the poet, who, when he made it back to Indianapolis, lived for a time at the Denison House. "I am getting tired of this way of living— clean, dead tired, and fagged out and sick of the whole Bohemian business," lamented Riley. There are a number of stories about how the poet abandoned his footloose existence for life in the

Holstein home. According to Riley biographer Marcus Dickey, the Hoosier author boldly announced after dinner one night with the Holsteins the following: "I am never coming back again except on one condition." When a perplexed Holstein asked what that condition might be, Riley replied: "That I come as a boarder." Another version, from Riley's niece Mrs. Harry Miesse, involved a mix-up during a vacation at French Lick. By mischance, all of Riley's luggage was sent to the Holstein house in Indianapolis, and the poet decided he might as well make his home there.

However Riley happened to decide to live as a paying guest with the Holsteins, he soon settled comfortably into his new surroundings. Katie Kindell, who served as housekeeper during Riley's residence there, noted that the poet often wrote in bed as much as at a desk, always keeping paper and pencil close by in case an idea for a poem might come to mind. His advice to young writers, said Kindell, was to "use the rubber end of your pencil as much as the point. Write and rewrite." The Holsteins' cook, Nannie Ewing, recalled that Riley often came to the kitchen to thank her when he

enjoyed a meal, especially when the meal included his favorites, pumpkin or sweet potato pie. "Sometimes he would slip a little piece of money in my hand," said Ewing. "Most times, he would make up verses about the food and recite them to me as he stood in the doorway. When I laughed at them he was satisfied, and would go up to his room, chuckling as he went."

Riley also made his presence known to his Lockerbie neighbors. Earl McKee, who lived with his family in a house at the corner of Lockerbie and East Streets, noted that most of the children in the area had "at least a speaking acquaintance with Riley, and he frequently was an interested spectator at our more spectacular activities," standing and watching a marble game sometimes for as long as a half hour and offering humorous comments on the match. The poet knew all the youngsters' names but, according to McKee, took "huge delight in addressing each boy by the wrong name. We were slightly in awe of the poet and seldom had the temerity to correct his apparent lapse of memory."

The Holstein home became a regular visiting place for Indiana schoolchildren and for famous figures like perennial Socialist presidential candidate and labor organizer Eugene Debs, who enjoyed raising a glass of spirits with Riley whenever possible. The poet's fame grew so great that his birthday was celebrated by students throughout the country. After his death, which came as he slept in his room in the Holstein residence on the evening of 22 July 1916, more than thirty-five thousand people filed past his casket as it lay in state under the dome at the Indiana State Capitol in Indianapolis.

Through the foresight of a group of Riley friends that included George Ade, William C. Bobbs, William Fortune, George C. Hitt, Meredith Nicholson, and Booth Tarkington, the house the poet called home for so many years was acquired by Fortune from the estate of Mrs. Charles L. Holstein following her death on 18

October 1916. The James Whitcomb Riley Memorial Association, which was organized in 1921, purchased the property from Fortune and opened the house as a public museum in 1922 with Kindell as its first hostess. The association later constructed a children's hospital and a summer camp for young people with physical disabilities as memorials to the poet.

Described as one of the finest Victorian preservations in the country, the James Whitcomb Riley Home features numerous furnishings and other household goods from Riley's days in the house. The poet's room includes some of his clothing and a Wayman Adams painting of his cherished poodle, Lockerbie. The library contains Riley's easy chair, his book collection and that of the Nickum and Holstein families, and portraits of Riley and his friend Joel Chandler Harris, author of the Uncle Remus stories. In the drawing room is an Apollo electric player piano, a gift to the poet from its manufacturer, Melville Clark. A niece of Riley said her uncle "thought it great fun" to play the piano while she accompanied him on her violin.

Located near downtown Indianapolis, the Riley home is open from 10:00 A.M. to 4:00 P.M. Tuesday through Saturday and noon to 4:00 P.M. on Sunday. For more information, write the site at 528 Lockerbie St., Indianapolis, IN 46202; or call (317) 631-5885.

Riley's boyhood home in Greenfield remained in the Riley family until 1935, when it was sold to the city of Greenfield by Julia Riley, James Whitcomb Riley's sister-in-law. Two years later the Riley Old Home Society was formed to assist in preserving the home as a memorial to Greenfield's favorite son. In 1972 the city also purchased the adjoining home, the John Mitchell home, to house historically significant memorabilia of Riley, Greenfield, and Hancock County. For more information on the Riley home in Greenfield, write the site at 250 W. Main St., Greenfield, IN 46140; or call (317) 462-8539.

RUTHMERE MANSION

In the 1880s in the northern Indiana town of Elkhart, Dr. Franklin Miles, an eye and ear specialist who had received his medical training from Rush Medical College, began to market a host of home remedies to consumers through his Dr. Miles Medical Company. Products marketed by the Elkhart physician included the popular Dr. Miles' Nervine, a sedative to be taken by those suffering from "nervousness or nervous exhaustion, sleeplessness, hysteria, headache, neuralgia, backache, pain, epilepsy, spasms, fits, St. Vitus' dance." The company's fortunes improved in 1889 when two successful local businessmen, George Compton and Albert R. Beardsley (known by all as A. R.), joined the firm.

Beardsley, who became general manager in 1890, was a member of a family significant in Elkhart's history. In 1832 Dr. Havilah Beardsley, Albert Beardsley's uncle, opened a gristmill on the north bank of the Saint Joseph River and platted the village of Elkhart along the south bank. The Beardsley name is perhaps best known in Elkhart today, however, because of the impressive three-story mansion built between 1908 and 1910 for A. R. and his wife, Elizabeth: Ruthmere. Named for the couple's only child, Ruth, who died in infancy, the structure, designed by architect Enock Hill Turnock, combines the elaborate formality of the Beaux Arts style with the more functional midwestern Prairie school of architecture. After an extensive renovation sponsored by the Andrew Hubble Beardsley Foundation, Ruthmere opened to the public as a house museum in 1973 with Indiana governor Otis R. Bowen presiding.

Born in Dayton, Ohio, on 7 November 1847, Albert Beardsley had a simple common-school education. While he was in his early teens, he moved to Elkhart to live with his aunt, Rachel Calhoun Beardsley, the widow of the community's founder. A. R. earned his keep by rising each morning to milk his aunt's cows. To help clothe himself, he did chores for neighbors, including sawing wood at fifty cents a cord. In 1864 Beardsley began work as an apprentice clerk in John Davenport's dry goods store. Five years later, with a $250 gift from his father, A. R. opened his own dry goods store and through the years became one of Elkhart's leading merchants. In 1876 he left the dry goods business and acquired stock in the Muzzy Starch Company, becoming president of the firm in 1882.

Beardsley enjoyed great success in politics as well. A staunch Republican, he started his political career on the local level, serving as city clerk, city treasurer, and councilman. By 1899 Beardsley was ready for statewide office, winning election as state representative from Elkhart County. He went on to serve two terms (1905 and 1907) in the state senate. In his history of the Indiana Republican party, Russel Seeds praised Beardsley as "one of the most conservative and able members of that body [the legislature]." While in the assembly Beardsley sponsored bills for the creation and upkeep of good roads for the state and a measure prohibiting the use of live pigeons in shooting matches. The latter passed the senate but was defeated in the house.

The Elkhart entrepreneur also found time to pursue other, more personal, matters. On 24 September 1872 Beardsley married Elizabeth Florence Baldwin. The wedding proved to be a surprise to the community. "The matter was kept an almost perfect secret," reported the *Elkhart Evening Review*, "only a few friends being admitted to a knowledge of the event until it was a matter of the past. The wedding was a quiet affair, only a few guests being present." After honeymooning in New York, the couple returned to Elkhart and settled into a house at 307 West High Street. In December 1880 Elizabeth Beardsley gave birth to a daughter, named Ruth. Tragically, the infant was afflicted with hydrocephalus, an abnormal increase in the amount of fluid within the cranial cavity. The baby died in July 1881; the Beardsleys never had another child.

The parents were able to keep their daughter's name alive, however. When the Beardsleys started building a new home along the bank of the Saint Joseph River in 1908, they decided to name it Ruthmere: Ruth, after their beloved child, and *mere*, meaning near the water. For the design of their new home, the Beardsleys retained the services of English-born Turnock. Turnock, who attended grammar school and high school in Elkhart, had received training at the Art Institute of Chicago in the 1880s. After working for several years

in the offices of architect William Le Baron Jenney, Turnock opened a firm in 1890, practicing first in Chicago and then in Elkhart after 1907. He is best known for designing the Brewster Apartments, now a Chicago landmark. In Elkhart, Turnock received commissions for a number of municipal buildings, churches, factories, and homes for some of the community's leading citizens.

Upon hiring Turnock to plan his home, family legend has it that A. R. offered a few words of advice to the architect. "Whatever labor and material you buy," Beardsley is reported to have said, "try first to secure it in Elkhart. If you can't get them here, try the next county; if not the county then in Indiana, and if not the state then in America. Get everything as close to home as you can." Turnock listened to Beardsley's advice. When finished in 1910, Ruthmere included walnut woodwork believed to be from Elkhart County; limestone from Bedford, Indiana, quarries; yellow Belden brick from Canton, Ohio; and Cherokee marble from Georgia. An exception to Beardsley's rule was the extensive mahogany paneling in the house; it is reputed to be from Cuba. Also responsible for designing the home's interior, Turnock filled Ruthmere's rooms with silk upholstered wall coverings, intricately painted ceilings, and satin and velvet draperies. The cost for all of this is unknown, but one longtime Elkhart resident told a Beardsley descendant that her stonemason father once told her the mansion's perimeter walls alone cost $10,000—quite a sum for early-twentieth-century Indiana.

Along with its luxurious decor, the Elkhart mansion featured numerous innovations for its time. A Choralcello pipe organ, given to A. R. as a birthday present in 1918 and located in the entrance hall, could be played manually or with piano rolls. The music from the organ was piped into the first-floor library and the downstairs game room. The greenhouse is joined to the main house via an underground tunnel decorated with murals depicting scenes from the Italian lake country where the

Beardsleys often vacationed. Ruthmere may be one of the first private residences in the country to possess a fire-protection system and an air-purifying unit, which, unfortunately, never seemed to work properly. Even the garage had all the modern conveniences. Joseph Frazier, the Beardsleys' butler and driver, could pull the family's Detroit Edison electric car into the garage and park it on a turntable, which then could be cranked by hand so that the car would never have to be backed out.

By all accounts, the Beardsleys enjoyed their home, hosting numerous parties. Elizabeth Beardsley often received her guests wearing a hat and gloves while standing in front of the drawing-room fireplace. "She was gregarious and hearty," said Robert B. Beardsley, the couple's great-nephew who oversaw Ruthmere's restoration in the 1970s, "wore lipstick and heavy white powder when few women did, loved Worth perfume and tea roses, swore when she felt like it, and in later years drank a split of champagne (on doctor's orders) before going to bed."

The Beardsleys employed only two servants to look after Ruthmere, Frazier and Mary Tangborn, a maid and housekeeper. Childless, the Beardsleys showered their affection on

their pet chow named Wang. According to Robert Beardsley, the dog was known throughout the neighborhood for "his nasty disposition and the big red bow Aunt Elizabeth often made him wear."

With the Beardsleys' deaths in 1924 (they died within five months of each other), Arthur Beardsley, A. R.'s nephew and an officer with the Miles Company, purchased Ruthmere for $30,000. Upon his death in 1944 the home passed out of the family's hands, bought by a family with five young sons for $25,000. Through the years the property fell into disrepair. Seeing the building's plight, Robert Beardsley persuaded the Andrew Hubble Beardsley Foundation to acquire Ruthmere and restore it with the intention of opening it as a house museum. Beardsley hired O'Hara Decorating Service, Inc., of Chicago to conduct major portions of the restoration effort. Others consulted on the project included White House decorator Edwin K. Bitter and the National Trust for Historic Preservation. In saving the mansion, Robert Beardsley believed he was preserving "one of the finest examples of pre–World War I domestic architecture extant in the country. In addition, I wanted to show that houses like Ruthmere were found not only in Newport, Palm Beach, and the big coastal cities but in small towns as well." Later on he added his own touch by opening the Robert B. Beardsley Arts Reference Library of American Domestic Architecture and Decorative Arts, which is housed in the former chauffeur's quarters.

The restoration took five years and involved more than three hundred laborers, some of them earning as much as eighteen dollars an hour, an unbelievable figure compared to that received by the workers who originally built Ruthmere. While preparing the mansion's walls for new fabric, the renovators discovered pencil notations on the plaster from 1909. The figures showed fifty-two and a half hours of labor at the rate of twenty-seven cents an hour. In another part of the home, workers discovered that Elizabeth Beardsley, undertaking some redecorating before her death in 1924, had increased the rate of pay—an entry noted forty-eight hours of labor at sixty-seven cents an hour.

Open to the public since 1973, Ruthmere, which is listed on the National Register of Historic Places, is available for guided tours at 10:00 A.M., 11:00 A.M., 1:00 P.M., 2:00 P.M., and 3:00 P.M. Tuesday through Saturday from the first Tuesday in April through mid-December. Ruthmere is also open Sunday for 2:00 P.M. and 3:00 P.M. tours in July and August. Groups of five or more should call ahead for reservations. For more information, write Ruthmere at 302 E. Beardsley Ave., Elkhart, IN 46514; or call (219) 264-0330 or (888) 287-7696.

SEIBERLING MANSION

Kokomo's city fathers were thrilled. On 6 October 1886 in a cornfield owned by A. F. Armstrong, workers who had drilled down more than 920 feet finally found what they were looking for—a large natural gas vein that stretched in a gas belt through approximately nineteen Indiana counties. To capitalize on this discovery, city leaders quickly created an organization called the Citizens Free Gas Line for Factories Only, which enticed aspiring industrialists to the Howard County community by offering them free gas and free land. "Almost overnight," Ned Booher notes in his history of the city, "Kokomo was transformed from a rural trading center into an industrial hub." One of the first of the twenty-five entrepreneurs to take advantage of Kokomo's economic incentive package was Akron, Ohio, businessman Monroe Seiberling.

In 1887 Seiberling, who had manufactured everything from twine to plate glass during his residence in Akron, established the Kokomo Strawboard Company, which employed approximately seventy-five people to take ordinary straw and produce shoe boxes. Six months later Seiberling sold his company (at a profit) to the American Strawboard Company. Despite the sale, Seiberling remained in business in Kokomo, opening the Diamond Plate Glass Company. Although the onetime Ohio industrialist's Kokomo factories were impressive, he is best remembered for a more personal project: his family's home, which became known as the Seiberling Mansion. The structure, a mixture of Neo-Jacobean and Romanesque Revival styles built at a cost of $50,000, is today occupied by the Howard County Historical Society, which has restored the mansion for use as a museum.

Monroe Seiberling was born in 1839, the sixth of fifteen children raised on a farm in Summit City, Ohio, by Nathan and Catherine Seiberling. Seiberling's life reads much like a Horatio Alger story. After working on his father's farm until he was twenty-eight, he decided to move on and seek his fortune as a businessman in Akron. For the next fifteen years, Seiberling prospered through his involvement in the production of a wide range of materials, including twine, cordage, flour, rubber, plate glass, and strawboard. When Kokomo tapped into the famed Trenton Field of natural gas in 1886, however, Seiberling, attracted by the city's lucrative free land and gas offer, decided to pull up stakes and move his industrial expertise to the east-central Indiana area.

Although Seiberling established his factories in Kokomo by 1887, it took him another two years to decide upon a suitable site to build a home for his wife, Sarah, and their eight children—Alton, Emma, Kate, George, Laird, Fred, Grace, and Ella. In 1889 Seiberling purchased from David Spraker two acres known as Haskett's Grove, an area popular with picnickers and host to a number of political rallies through the years. Work on the home began in November 1889 with Arthur LaBelle of Marion as architect and I. V. Smith as contractor.

From the first, Smith found that Seiberling expected a lot

from his employees. Reminiscing about building the mansion, Smith related the following story to the *Kokomo Dispatch* in 1929: "Mr. Seiberling came to me about Nov. 1 and said, 'Ike, here is the plan for my home. I want it under roof come March 1.' I said to him, 'I don't think it can be done, as between those dates it is all winter.' He said, 'You go right at it.' So I did."

After Seiberling left the area to journey to New York on business, Smith came up with an ingenious solution to constructing a home during harsh winter weather. "As soon as he [Seiberling] was out of sight," said Smith, "I got lumber and built a house big enough so I could build a new house within it." It worked. All during the winter months construction continued on the home unimpeded by rain or snow. Seiberling was impressed by his contractor's quick thinking. "When Mr. Seiberling came home and saw what I had done, he patted me on the back and said, 'You are smarter than I thought you were,'" Smith recalled. Workmen dismantled the cocoon in March 1890, and local legend has it that Kokomo residents carried away from the site enough lumber to construct several buildings.

The mansion features arcade-style porches, a round tower with a cone-shaped roof, and amply sized rooms. The first floor includes

a library, music room, living room, and family breakfast room with a corner fireplace. All second-story rooms contain hand-carved fireplaces faced with white, gold, burgundy, and mulberry colored tile. A ballroom occupies the mansion's entire third floor and includes at its south end a platform on which entertainers could perform. To the platform's right is a large, cone-shaped, circular porch where guests could gather and admire the estate.

In 1895, with the Diamond Plate Glass Company's merger with the Pittsburgh Plate Glass Company, the Seiberling family left its palatial Kokomo mansion and moved to Peoria, Illinois, where Monroe Seiberling formed the Peoria Rubber and Manufacturing Company. In subsequent years the industrialist organized a plate glass company in Ottawa, Illinois, and was involved in mining projects in Nevada. He died at his Oak Park, Illinois, home on 28 February 1908. Following his death the *Kokomo Daily Tribune* memorialized the gas boom industrialist as "a likable, impulsive, generous, gifted man—one who liked to handle large affairs for the zest of the thing as much as for the profit."

In the years following the Seiberlings' departure from Kokomo, the mansion was owned by a number of people, includ-

ing George Kingston, who invented the Kingston Carburetor in 1902. In 1946 Indiana University at Kokomo purchased the home for $25,000, remodeling some rooms for use as classrooms. IU Kokomo used the mansion for approximately twenty years but moved out in 1965. The mansion stood empty until 1972, when the Howard County Historical Society announced plans for renovating the building for use as a museum, which was formally opened to the public on 12 August 1973. As part of Hoosier Celebration '88, the Kokomo community raised $275,000 to restore the mansion's interior and exterior. Committed to preserving and presenting the county's history, the Howard County Historical Society uses the Seiberling Mansion to display rotating exhibitions tracing the area's history. Also, several mansion rooms display period furnishings.

The Seiberling Mansion is open for tours from 1:00 P.M. to 4:00 P.M. Tuesday through Sunday. For more information, write the museum at 1200 W. Sycamore St., Kokomo, IN 46901; or call (765) 452-4314.

T. C. STEELE STATE HISTORIC SITE

On a spring day in 1907, two people, an Indiana artist well known for his portrait and landscape work and his bride-to-be, stood atop a hill overlooking Brown County's lush and wild landscape. The artist, who had expressed to his betrothed his need for a new location for his work, turned to her and proclaimed: "My dear, if you think you can manage to live in this wilderness, we will build our home here—on this hill." Anticipating the adventures that lay ahead for the couple, the young woman, whose brother had regaled her with tales about the area's "primitiveness and picturesqueness," told her future husband that living on the hilltop "could be made very simple, living so far away from everything—just among the trees and clouds."

Theodore Clement Steele, famed member along with William Forsyth, Otto Stark, Richard Gruelle, and J. Ottis Adams of the Hoosier Group of American regional impressionist painters, and Selma Neubacher Steele, the artist's second wife, went on to purchase 211 acres near Belmont in the Brown County hills. There they built their home, dubbed the House of the Singing Winds for the aural treats produced as the wind blew through the wire of the screened porches surrounding the house. The couple, married on 9 August 1907, later added a large studio to accommodate Steele's work, landscaped the surrounding hillsides, and created several acres of gardens encompassing the home. "We felt and believed," said Selma Steele, "that here in this hill country were evidences of character in the outdoors that would command of us our best and

finest spirit." Steele's estate, which includes his paintings, an eleven-room home, and a nine hundred-volume library, are all maintained as part of the T. C. Steele State Historic Site.

Honored during his career by election to the National Academy of Design and service as president of the Society of Western Artists, T. C. Steele was born in Owen County, Indiana, on 11 September 1847, the first child of Samuel and Harriett Steele. As a youth, Steele lived near

Waveland, a village he described as "a community of more than ordinary intelligence and situated in a charming and pleasant country of prosperous farms." Educated at the Waveland Collegiate Institute, Steele from an early age displayed an aptitude for drawing. By the age of thirteen he was teaching drawing at the institute, and five years later he was listed in the catalog for the school as the teacher of drawing and painting in the preparatory department.

Graduating in 1868, Steele went on to study painting for a brief time in Chicago and Cincinnati. In 1870 he married Mary Elizabeth "Libbie" Lakin, who had been a fellow student at the institute. Drawn by the promises of some painting commissions, the young couple lived in Battle Creek, Michigan, for a time before returning to the Hoosier State in 1873, settling in Indianapolis.

For Steele, as he confessed to his journal, the

two great qualities an artist had to possess to "pass the point of mediocrity" were mechanical skill matched with a "deep love of the beautiful." Struggling to live up to these qualities and make a living as an artist, Steele, through his work as a portrait painter, drew the attention and patronage of Indianapolis businessman Herman Lieber, who often exhibited the young painter's work in his store, the H. Lieber Company. Developing a reputation for his portrait work, Steele also won the attention of the local press. A reporter from the *Indianapolis Saturday Herald* described Steele as a "tall romantic-looking fellow" and as "an ideal artist in personal appearance, wearing his hair and whiskers long, after the manner of Bohemians generally." Steele, who in 1877 had joined with John Love to form the Indianapolis Art Association, left America in 1880 to study at the Royal Academy of Art in Munich, Germany, a trip sponsored by Lieber in association with other Indianapolis businessmen.

Upon his return to Indianapolis in 1885, Steele continued to earn his living as an artist, receiving commissions for portraits and also teaching art; for a time he worked with fellow Hoosier artist William Forsyth at the Indiana School of Art. Winning recognition as part of the Hoosier Group through an 1894 exhibition in Chicago, Steele stopped teaching a year later in order to devote more time to his work. Drawn more and more to landscape painting, he joined with J. Ottis Adams to purchase the Hermitage in Brookville. Writing to his daughter about the area, he

said that the "haze makes this country seem like some enchanted land, and as we ride about I feel more as if I were listening to some beautiful story and that my fancy was picturing it—that it was not real at all." Shortly after his appointment to a commission to select which American paintings were to be included in the Paris Universal Exposition, Steele suffered the loss of his wife, Libbie, who died on 14 November 1899 at the age of forty-nine.

His move to Brown County, and his marriage to Selma Neubacher, began a new phase in Steele's life and work. Writing to his fiancée as he supervised construction of their new home in

the hills in May 1907, Steele cautioned her not to expect too much from the property at the beginning of their life together. "Houses may be bought," he wrote, "but homes grow and out of the heart's depths. Memories cluster about them, so that when we give them up, there is a pain that will not go down. Rest and contentment and recreation live in the home, and out of it we get the inspiration and strength for the work in the world that tells. I look forward to this home for both of us, as a source of inspiration."

The location proved to be a boon for Steele's painting. Shortly after the newlyweds moved into their home, they settled on a routine. The morning was used for individual work—Selma Steele painted, too—and the afternoon for tramping around the countryside. "Before many days," she noted, "even this plan was broken—for the painter was overwhelmed by the number of paintable subjects to be done. Soon there were enough canvases started to cover the hours of almost the

entire day." The day began early for the artist, as he believed that during a "work season" no landscape painter should be in bed after four o'clock in the morning, his wife said. After an early lunch, Steele would rest for a short time, usually by reading, listening to music, or walking with his wife. Back to work in the afternoon and early evening, he often tramped far into the woods in order to capture the right subject. "I marveled at his capacity for work," Selma Steele said of her husband, adding that she came to realize that he possessed a rare gift. "It was like an inner flame that kept his whole being—mind, body, and soul—ever alive to the shifting scenes around him," she observed.

From 1907 to 1921 the Steeles spent the spring season at their Brown County property and wintered in Indianapolis. In 1922, when T. C. Steele became artist in residence and an honorary professor at Indiana University, the couple established a

home in Bloomington. While working on a painting of a peony arrangement at his Brown County home in May 1926, Steele fell seriously ill. After a trip to a clinic in Terre Haute failed to offer any relief, the Steeles returned to their home on the hill on the Fourth of July. The painter died at eight o'clock in the evening on 24 July 1926. For comfort, Selma Steele recalled something her husband had once said to her during a time of sorrow: "Don't you know there are some things one cannot reason out?"

After her husband's death Selma Steele continued to improve the Brown County property, in hopes that it would be an "ever-unfailing source of inspiration." In 1934 she bought a two-story, two-room cabin and had it moved onto the estate. The cabin had been built in approximately 1871 by Peter Dewar, a Scottish immigrant, as a wedding present for his son. In the spring of 1945 Selma Steele donated the prop-

erty and more than three hundred paintings by her husband to the State of Indiana as a memorial to the artist. Today, the T. C. Steele State Historic Site offers guided tours through the House of the Singing Winds and the Large Studio where changing exhibitions display paintings done throughout Steele's life. The site also includes five hiking trails, the Dewar Log Cabin, and the ninety-two-acre Selma Steele Nature Preserve.

The T. C. Steele State Historic Site is located one and a half miles south of Belmont, off Highway 46, nine miles west of Nashville and ten miles east of Bloomington. It is open from 9:00 A.M. to 5:00 P.M. Tuesday through Saturday and 1:00 P.M. to 5:00 P.M. on Sunday. The site is closed mid-December to mid-March. For more information, write the site at 4220 T. C. Steele Rd., Nashville, IN 47448; or call (812) 988-2785.

Wandering through the fields on her father's farm one morning, a young Wabash County girl heard a gunshot, looked up, and spied a large bird plummeting to earth. Running to the spot where the bird fell, she discovered a chicken hawk with a badly broken wing and her father who was preparing to club the injured animal with his rifle. Distraught, the girl, already known by her neighbors as a nature lover, beseeched her father to give her the hawk to nurse back to health. Her father angrily gave in to her wishes, responding: "God knows I do not understand you. Keep the bird if you think you can!" The girl's father, a minister, watched in amazement over the weeks as the bird recovered and devotedly began to follow the child around the farm. Impressed, the preacher gave all the birds on the family's property to his daughter as a gift. "Even while he was talking to me," the girl recalled, "I was making a flashing mental inventory of my property, for now I owned the hummingbirds, dressed in green satin with ruby jewels on their throats; the plucky little brown wren that sang by the hour to his mate from the top of the pump, even in a hard rain; the green warbler nesting in . . . wild sweetbriar beside the back porch; and the song sparrow in the ground cedar beside the fence."

The affinity for nature shown by the Hoosier child expressed itself in other ways as the girl matured to womanhood. Through such books as *Freckles*, *A Girl of the Limberlost*, *Laddie*, and *Michael O'Halloran*, Gene Stratton-Porter won popular acclaim and, in time, came to believe that she was a latter-day Moses, leading the women of her day back to nature and away from the strictures imposed on them by society. She had some success; an estimated fifty million people have read her work, and her books have been translated into several foreign languages. By the time she died in a Los Angeles, California, traffic accident on 6 December 1924, she had become, as Yale pundit William Lyon Phelps termed her, "a public institution, like Yellowstone Park." The memory of one of the leading lights of Indiana's golden age of literature is maintained by two sites in the state, the Limberlost Cabin in Geneva, where Stratton-Porter braved the treacherous Limberlost Swamp and wrote six novels and five nature books, and the Cabin in Wildflower Woods on Sylvan Lake in Rome City, where she lived and worked from 1914 to 1919.

Born on a farm in Wabash County, Indiana, on 17 August 1863, Geneva Grace Stratton was the youngest of twelve children. Her father, Mark Stratton, was a licensed Methodist minister and prosperous farmer. Her mother, Mary (Shallenberger) Stratton, became ill when Gene was five years old and died in 1875. While Gene had little formal schooling in her early years, she developed a lively interest in nature and wildlife at an early age. "By the day I trotted from one object which attracted me to another," she noted, "singing a little song of made-up phrases about everything I saw while I waded catching fish, chasing butterflies over clover fields, or following a bird with a hair in its beak." When her family moved to the city of Wabash in 1874, she began to attend school on a regular basis and completed all but the last term of high school.

On 21 April 1886 Gene married Charles D. Porter, a druggist and banker, who was thirteen years her senior. Living for a short time in Decatur, the couple moved to Geneva after the birth of their daughter, Jeannette, in 1887. "I did not write," Gene Stratton-Porter said of her early days of marriage, "but I continued violin, painting and embroidery lessons, and did all the cooking and housework with the exception of the washing and ironing. I had agreed to love a man, and to keep his house neat and clean." She did maintain her connection with nature by keeping several different kinds of birds in her household. After oil was discovered on some farmland owned by Charles Porter, Gene Stratton-Porter used the new family wealth to

construct in 1895 a fourteen-room, Queen Anne rustic-style home on the outskirts of town near the vast Limberlost Swamp.

Encompassing approximately thirteen thousand acres in southern Adams County and northern Jay County, the Limberlost won for itself a reputation as a "treacherous swamp and quagmire, filled with every plant, animal and human danger known—in the worst of such locations in the central states." According to legend the swamp received its name from the fate of Limber Jim Corbus, who went hunting in the swamp and became lost for some time. When local residents asked where Jim Corbus had gone, the familiar answer was "Limber's lost!" The swamp was where Stratton-Porter began to photograph birds and animals in their natural habitat. She sent her photographs, with no explanation, to *Recreation* magazine. Impressed by her efforts, the periodical asked her to write a camera column and paid her with new photographic equipment. A year later, *Outing* magazine hired her to do similar work.

Encouraged by these accomplishments, Stratton-Porter turned to writing fiction. Her first novel, *The Song of the Cardinal*, illustrated with photographs by the author, met with modest success,

but her next book, *Freckles*, established her tremendous popularity with the reading public, selling more than 670,000 copies in ten years. Although her sentimental style won favor with her readers, Stratton-Porter's work never received much critical acclaim, a fact that puzzled her. She asked why the "life history of the sins and shortcomings of a man should constitute a book of realism, and the life history of a just and incorruptible man should constitute a book of idealism. Is not a moral man as real as an immoral one?"

In 1913, with the Limberlost Swamp drained and cleared for farming and commercial ventures, Stratton-Porter and her fam-

ily moved to northern Indiana, where she built a new home—the Cabin in Wildflower Woods—on the shores of Sylvan Lake at Rome City. She was attracted to the lakefront site by a wood duck she spied near the shore and an acre of blue-eyed grass on the property. "I bought the wood duck and the blue-eyed grass, with a wealth of tall hardwood trees for good measure," she said. Stratton-Porter took a personal interest in the construction of her new home, noting that she was on the job "from the drawing of the line for the back steps between the twin oaks to the last stroke of polish that finished the floors." The Hoosier author also

worked with Frank Wallace, a tree surgeon and later Indiana State Entomologist, to improve the 150-acre property.

In 1919 Stratton-Porter relocated to California, where she took on for *McCall's* magazine a monthly column, which first appeared in January 1922. In addition to her writing, she also organized her own movie company and based a number of her films on her best-selling books. "As a motion picture producer," Stratton-Porter told her *McCall's* readers, "I shall continue to present idealized pictures of life, pictures of men and women who inspire charity, honor, devotion to God and to family." At age sixty-

one Stratton-Porter was killed in an automobile accident just a few blocks from her Los Angeles home. She was buried in Hollywood Cemetery in California. For many years, her last wish went unfulfilled. It was: "When I am gone, I hope my family will bury me out in the open, and plant a tree on my grave; I do not want a monument. A refuge for a bird nest is all the marker I want."

In May 1999 Stratton-Porter's last wish came true as her remains, and those of her daughter Jeannette, were interred at her home on Sylvan Lake near Rome City. In addition to the author's gravesite, the Gene Stratton-Porter State Historic Site

maintains the gardens, arbor, orchard, and scenic paths surrounding the Cabin in Wildflower Woods. The site encompasses 34 of the property's original 150 acres and holds many of Stratton-Porter's furnishings and personal memorabilia. Donated to the State of Indiana in 1947, the fourteen-room Limberlost Cabin, also a state historic site, includes many furnishings used by Stratton-Porter and her family. The Limberlost site also includes the Loblolly Marsh Wetland Preserve, a 428-acre preserve that is being restored to reflect the Limberlost Swamp area described by Stratton-Porter in her work.

The Limberlost State Historic Site is located one block east of U.S. 27 on Sixth Street in Geneva. The Gene Stratton-Porter State Historic Site (the Cabin in Wildflower Woods) is located at 1205 Pleasant Point in Rome City. Both sites are open mid-March through mid-December from 9:00 A.M. to 5:00 P.M. Tuesday through Saturday and 1:00 P.M. to 5:00 P.M. on Sunday. For more information, write the Limberlost site at P.O. Box 356, Geneva, IN 46740; or call (219) 368-7428. Write the Gene Stratton-Porter State Historic Site at P.O. Box 639, Rome City, IN 46784; or call (219) 854-3790.

The U.S. minister to Turkey in 1885 found himself in a quandary. He had just prepared a telegram offering his resignation to Democratic president Grover Cleveland, whose party affiliation he did not share. Writing to his wife back home in Crawfordsville about his plans for the future, he told her that he was sure he would not be going back to his old law practice, terming it "the most detestable of human occupations." Instead, he dreamed of building a study where he could "write, and . . . think of nothing else. I want to bury myself in a den of books. I want to saturate myself with the elements of which they are made and breathe their atmosphere until I am of it. Not a book worm . . . but a man in the world of writing—one with a pen which shall stop men to listen to it, whether they wish to or not."

Lew Wallace got his wish. More than a decade after sharing his dream of a study with his wife, Susan, Wallace began building in Crawfordsville what *The Chariot* magazine called "a harmonious mingling of Romanesque, Greek and Byzantine architecture." The study, which contributed greatly to Crawfordsville's designation as the Athens of Indiana, is maintained today as the General Lew

Wallace Study and Ben-Hur Museum. The study and grounds, once part of the Maj. Isaac Compton Elston estate, were declared a National Historic Landmark by the federal government in 1977.

The study's eclectic architectural mix matched the remarkable diversity of its builder's own career. At various times in his life Wallace was a lawyer; Indiana state senator; major general during the Civil War; vice president of the court-martial that tried the conspirators behind the assassination of President Abraham Lincoln; New Mexico Territory governor; American minister to Turkey from 1881 to 1885; and, the role for which he is best remembered today, author of the classic historical novel *Ben-Hur: A Tale of the Christ*. One of Wallace's biographers, Irving McKee, noted in his book *"Ben-Hur" Wallace* that the Hoosier Renaissance man was "never content with the ordinary business of existence—working for dollars, rearing a family, snatching at comforts and petty advantages. He dreamed grandly of adventure and sought it, adventure fit for the American hero as well as the foreign knight."

Wallace's grand dream of what he called "a pleasure-house for my soul" came to life in Crawfordsville, where he and his wife had lived on and off since 1853. The study's construction began in 1896 and was finished three years later at a cost of $35,000. Working under specifications drawn up by Wallace himself, architect John C. Thurtle produced what one newspaper called "the most beautiful author's study in the world . . . a dream of oriental beauty and luxury."

The study featured a dizzying array of architectural styles, including an entrance modeled on the abbey of the church of Saint Pierre in France; a forty-foot-high tower with arched windows designed from the Cathedral of Pisa; and a copper dome and stained-glass skylight that reflected the mosques Wallace had come to know while U.S. minister to Turkey. Also, a limestone frieze, which included likenesses of characters from Wallace's novels, ran around the tower and study. Although the building elicited a mixed critical reaction, the study was perfect for Wallace. According to McKee, "its eclecticism is American yet foreign, as Wallace was American yet foreign; he loved passionately his country and his State, yet lusted for distant, unattainable realms."

Wallace had only a short time to enjoy the stately structure he created, dying at his Crawfordsville home on 15 February 1905. Before his final illness, the Civil War veteran had noted the passing of a fellow soldier by commenting: "He is but a day's march ahead of us; we will overtake him soon." Following Wallace's death his beloved study was under the care of his family. In 1941, however, the Community House, an organization established by the women of Crawfordsville, purchased the study and grounds from Lewis Wallace, the general's grandson, and presented

the property to the city for use as a memorial to Wallace's life.

Today, the study, which is maintained by the city's Park and Recreation Department, features an impressive array of Wallace memorabilia. The three and a half acres of grounds surrounding the study include a bronze statue of Wallace, which is a duplicate of the one in the U.S. Capitol in Washington, D.C. The statue is west of the study and stands in place of a beech tree under which Wallace wrote much of *Ben-Hur*. The grounds also feature a monument to Wallace's father, David Wallace, who was Indiana's sixth governor.

The inside of the study features such relics from Wallace's career as the arms, shield, and charm taken from an Apache chief who was killed by Wallace's bodyguards when the general was on an

AUTHOR

inspection tour while governor of the New Mexico Territory; a sword presented to Wallace by his fellow Montgomery County citizens in honor of his gallantry at the Battle of Fort Donelson; a horseshoe from Old John, Wallace's war horse; a Confederate cavalry flag captured during the Battle of Monocacy and solid shot from that battlefield; and a complete outfit for a Roman soldier, including cape, helmet, armor, and sandals, used in the 1959 movie *Ben-Hur*.

The General Lew Wallace Study and Ben-Hur Museum is open from 1:00 P.M. to 4:30 P.M. Tuesday through Sunday (1 April through 31 October). During June, July, and August the museum opens at 10:00 A.M. on Wednesday through Saturday. For more information, write the site at 501 W. Pike St., Crawfordsville, IN 47933; or call (765) 362-5769.